D1714370

Flannery O'Connor

In Celebration of Genius

Flannery O'Connor

In Celebration of Genius

EDITED BY

SARAH GORDON

Hill Street Press **d** Athens, Georgia

A HILL STREET PRESS BOOK

Published in the United States of America by
Hill Street Press LLC
191 East Broad Street, Suite 209
Athens, Georgia 30601-2848 USA
706-613-7200
info@hillstreetpress.com www.hillstreetpress.com

Hill Street Press is committed to preserving the written word.
Every effort is made to print books on acid-free paper
with a significant amount of post-consumer recycled content.

Text and cover design by Anne Richmond Boston.

Printed in the United States of America.

Library of Congress Cataloging-in-Publication Data

Flannery O'Connor : in celebration of genius / edited by Sarah Gordon.
       p.   cm.
     ISBN 1-892514-66-4 (alk. paper)
     1. O'Connor, Flannery—Criticism and interpretation. 2. O'Connor,
Flannery—Influence. 3. Women and literature—Southern States—
History—20th century. I. O'Connor, Flannery. II. Gordon, Sarah, 1941–

     PS3565.C57 Z66784 2000
     813'.54—dc21
                                        00-023200

ISBN # 1-892514-66-4
10   9   8   7   6   5   4   3   2   1
First printing

In memory of Mary Flannery O'Connor
on the occasion of the seventy-fifth anniversary of her birth
March 25, 2000

Contents

Preface

Like many other contributors to this tribute volume, I have bean reading Flannery O'Connor's fiction for years—thirty-three, in fact. While I am aghast at the swift passage of the years, I am even more shocked by my own lasting fascination with O'Connor's work. In 1963, when I began working on an undergraduate honors project in fiction at Randolph-Macon Woman's College, my advisor and mentor suggested that I read O'Connor, "that writer from Milledgeville who raises peacocks." My teacher predicted that I would like O'Connor and that I could learn something from her. Swept up, however, in the whirling excitement of my senior year and undoubtedly heady with the certainty of my own vision (as only college seniors can be), I failed to read the Georgia writer. I did finish my honors thesis, a series of short stories, but I had certainly missed the opportunity of learning from a real master. In August of 1964, several months after my graduation, I read of O'Connor's death at age thirty-nine. Death at such an early age! I was horrified by the loss, feeling strangely (and selfishly) cheated, for the newspaper and magazine accounts of her talent intrigued me. I decided to follow up on my reading assignment, however belatedly.

I was hooked on first reading. As a Southerner transplanted to Missouri, I thought O'Connor had captured the South in a wildly humorous and deeply authentic manner. O'Connor's sharp, sometimes menacing descriptions, her brilliant juxtapositions and sense of timing, and her keen ear for the language of banality attracted me initially: I roared laughing, and, to tell the truth, I haven't stopped yet. Surely, I thought, I had never read anything like this work. Where did it come from? Who was this Georgia writer? I have been seeking the answers to those questions and many others ever since. For twenty-five yeas I have been teaching at Georgia College & State University, O'Connor's alma mater, the repository of her manuscripts and private library and thus the center for O'Connor studies in the world. Those of us who work in O'Connor studies at our institution have watched as O'Connor's reputation has grown, both nationally and internationally, from the early days of reader bafflement to the present time in which O'Connor's popularity soars. She is even lauded by rock stars like Bruce Springsteen, cartoonists like Matt Groening, actors like Holly Hunter and Tommy Lee Jones, and discussed on radio and television as one of the preeminent writers of the short story in English. Scholarly interest in her work has increased monumentally since her death, and even though she might be surprised at some of the "takes" on her fiction, O'Connor can rest assured that—contrary to her prediction—she won't have to wait a hundred years to be understood.

When Judy Long of Hill Street Press asked me to edit a collection of tributes from contemporary writers for the celebration of the anniversary of O'Connor's seventy-fifth birthday on March 25, 2000, I was delighted. When I learned that royalties from the sale of books would benefit

The O'Connor Collection at the Ina Dillard Russell Library, I was extremely gratified. We sought out writers who we believed had been influenced by or in some large way affected by O'Connor's work and life. Some writers whose "voices" we would have liked to have heard were committed to other projects and genuinely regretted not having the time to dedicate to this book—Alice Munro, Sally Fitzgerald, and Horton Foote, for example—while others eagerly complied. The writers included in this volume willingly agreed to write about O'Connor's place in their creative lives and donate their royalties to The O'Connor Collection at our university. The assistance of the staff of The O'Connor Collection, and in particular that of Nancy Davis Bray, has proven to be invaluable on this project.

This volume is, I believe, a genuine reflection of the diversity of O'Connor's influence, as well as an indication that O'Connor continues to make a strong impact on young writers. Kellie Wells, for example, a young fiction writer whose work received special mention for the Pushcart Prize, writes of the gifts her fiction has received from O'Connor, and Susan Elizabeth Howe, a fine poet from Utah, recounts in "A Scholar Goes to Milledgeville" the appropriateness of the journey to its destination. Well established writers are also represented here. Fred Chappell testifies to the dizzying effect of a dose of O'Connor's "dangerous" fiction, and Madison Jones places O'Connor's spiritual values and her stylistic brilliance within the context of the Fugitive movement and its concern with morality and tradition. The one exception to this volume's emphasis on O'Connor's influence on writers is the tribute of Guerrilla Girl Alma Thomas, a visual artist. On a recent trip to the GC&SU campus, Thomas (as her piece indicates this not her real name) toured the O'Connor Collection and told me she had replaced her copy of *Mystery and Manners* four times, so marked did each copy become as she read and reread the book. On impulse, I told her of this project and asked if she would consider writing something, and she most graciously agreed. Perhaps the most moving piece in this collection is that of Nancy Mairs, a fine writer of creative nonfiction who has suffered for years from multiple sclerosis. Mairs' letter to Flannery is a loving tribute to another writer who, though suffering from debilitating physical problems, nonetheless persevered.

O'Connor's fiction, her essays, and her letters continue to challenge and to illuminate the lives of all kinds of readers. Some of them, such as Bret Lott and David Madden, wrestle with her work and her ideas; others find her—shall I use the word?—inspirational. As for this reader, O'Connor's work *reads me* like that of few others. There is much in me of Hazel Motes, Joy/Hulga Hopewell, and other inhabitants of O'Connor's absurd but strangely familiar world. Like Thomas Merton, when I think of the work of Flannery O'Connor, I think not of "Hemingway or Katherine Anne Porter, but rather of someone like Sophocles." Merton adds, "What more can you say for a writer? I write her name with honor, for all the truth and all the craft with which she shows man's fall and his dishonor."

Flannery O'Connor: In Celebration of Genius is our way of acknowledging the *genius*—the very present spirit—of Flannery O'Connor. We are all profoundly grateful for her life and work.

Sarah Gordon
Milledgeville, Georgia

One

Remembering Flannery O'Connor

In the fall of 1957 I turned from the teaching of biology to become a traveling representative for a New York publisher of college textbooks and settled with my family in Macon, Georgia, the town most nearly at the center of my territory. I had no idea at the time, of course, what a richly rewarded move it would be.

Traveling with my bag of books, I always sought out on the various campuses the faculty I most wanted to know, meeting and forming lasting friendships, especially with James Dickey, Randall Jarrell, and Robert Lowell (who was often Jarrell's houseguest in North Carolina). Flannery O'Connor was not on the faculty at Georgia College, but I was not going to let that simple fact keep me from meeting one of the finest writers of fiction in English in our time— fiction published, I was pleased to note, by the company whose car had taken me to Milledgeville.

I asked for directions, drove to the farm, knocked on the

door, and introduced myself as a Harcourt Brace representative, come to say hello since I was in the neighborhood. I was as surprised as I was honored, delighted, and frightened when Flannery asked me onto the wide, screened-in front porch, where we sat in wicker rockers and talked for a while. I told her that my visit actually had nothing to do with Harcourt Brace, that I was a salesman with the text division of the company, and that I had just used the connection as a pretext to speak with her.

"I know," she said.

I told her that I was a poet.

"I thought so," she said.

At her invitation, I began to drive over from Macon at least once a month—whenever I was off the road—often taking along my four-year-old daughter Lucinda, who laughed and fell and laughed and fell again as she chased Flannery's peacocks. When I scolded her for it, Flannery told me to let her go.

"She won't catch them unless they want her to."

Usually Flannery and I would sit on the porch and talk as we watched the wide-circling race in the great yard, drinking iced tea that her mother would bring us, accompanied by a saucer of small watermelon cubes, each with a toothpick handle. I quickly came to love Flannery as a dear and dying friend.

Sometimes she would give me one or two books of poetry that had been sent to her, sometimes by the poet, saying that she didn't know how to read poems. She read mine, though, and commented on them sensibly and helpfully. I suspected that the real reason she passed the books along was that she didn't have room for them on her shelves and knew that I couldn't have afforded them.

"You know how to read poems," I insisted. "You write poems. You just call them stories."

"You write stories," she countered, grinning. "They just look like poems."

From the moment she turned my remark around and handed it back to me, my attitude toward my work was never the same.

Other things she said to me on those Saturday afternoons have stayed on the walls of my head like brief memos, never to be moved or covered up by later hands. I see them whenever I browse there:

* *Tell the truth, but understand that it is not necessarily what happened.*

* *Every good story is a parable.*

* *Don't let anyone or anything cut into your time with words.*
  (One Saturday when I drove onto the property twenty minutes earlier than I was expected, the shades on the windows of her room were lowered as the car pulled to a stop and I stayed inside it until they went up again.)

* *When I mentioned that all of my academic work had been in the sciences, with only three hours of freshman English on my transcripts, saying that I never took a course that would teach me to be a poet, she said, "Yes, you did."*
  "For instance?" I asked her.
  "Every one of them."

🌵 *We were not on the porch but at Agnes Scott College when she sat on a panel with John Ciardi and others, discussing and fielding questions about literature. She was asked by a young woman in the audience if college writing courses discouraged young people who might otherwise become writers.*

"Oh," she answered, "not nearly enough of them."

The lupus didn't enter often into our conversation, but she told me once when we were talking about the discovery and exploration of new work, "I don't have a lot of time. I can give a poem a couple of lines, a short story a paragraph, and a novel a few pages, then if I can stop reading without a sense of loss, I do, and I go on to something else."

When the head of the English Department at Louisiana State University wanted me to join the faculty in 1962, bringing with me all three hours of freshmen composition along with my doctoral work in physiology and needed some way to convince the dean that he was not delusional, it was in great part a letter from Milledgeville that did it.

Rather than rambling further, let me say simply and gladly that whatever I am as a writer and as a person, or whatever I am not, I am much more than I would have been without Flannery O'Connor's friendship, faith, and almost puckish counsel. A photograph of her with her crutches, standing on the brick steps of the front porch and smiling down at one of the peacocks, hangs on the wall of my study so that I can see it as I type this. I still miss her.

Miller Williams

Two

Dear Flannery,

P lease pardon the informality of my address. Both our mothers—Anne the New England Protestant and Regina the Southern Catholic—would have frowned on such quick familiarity, I'm sure. But having recently spent long hours in your presence through the letters compiled by your friend Sally Fitzgerald in *The Habit of Being*, I feel as though I've joined the company of friends to whom you posted the details—now practical, now intellectual, now spiritual—of your foreshortened life. True, the intimacy is grotesquely one-sided, since you are currently dead and I am not, but perhaps death has less power to divide us than our circumstances might once have had.

I doubt that we'd have been friends in your lifetime. Your death, on August 3, 1964, followed hard upon my graduation from college and my twenty-first birthday, and you had written, just weeks before, that "the young are a trial to listen to.

I'm very intolerant of them." I'd have been especially insufferable in those days, a positive fount of prattle, all but empty of content and with a faintly hysterical edge, designed to screen the black hole of depression that consumed my core.

You weren't very much older, with a B.A. from Georgia State College for Women and an M.F.A. from the State University of Iowa, when *The Habit of Being* opens in 1948 with a letter to a prospective agent. No babble or dither here. You already knew, as Sally Fitzgerald points out, just what you "could and wanted to do": write. Just as I did. The difference—and it is all the difference in the world—is that you were already acting on your desire and would continue to do so until your death, producing two novels and thirty-one short stories as well as reviews, essays, addresses, and, of course, this voluminous correspondence. Toward the end, able to write only an hour a day, you wrote, "[M]y I like to work. I et up that one hour like it was filet mignon." You practiced the discipline you enjoined upon a friend enduring a dry spell: "Just write every day whether you know what you're doing or not." And later: "You ought to spend three hours every morning in which you write or do nothing else: no reading, no talking, no cooking, no nothing, but you sit there." Fortunate friend!

The most important element in your life, at the time you were living it, would have struck me as utterly alien: your Southernness, your Catholicism, your disability. Although the year before you died I chanced to spend the summer in Georgia, I couldn't make any sense whatsoever of the Southern experience. Still can't. "I sure am sick of the Civil War," you wrote. That's the simplest way to tell the difference between the Southern writer and the Northern, I've decided: You got a bellyful of the Civil War while I hardly knew it had occurred. I grew awfully weary of The Flight from the Papists, however. We're all bound to be ghost-ridden one way or another.

Years later, I ceased fleeing the Papists and embraced them, though not necessarily in ways with which you'd have agreed. Still, because you wrote to a friend struggling against conversion, "I think most people come to the Church by means the Church does not allow," you might have tolerated more divergence than I give you credit for. Certainly, even though you could "never have the experience of the convert or of the one who fails to be converted," you grasped a fundamental distinction between Protestantism and Catholicism: "You don't join the Catholic Church. You *become* a Catholic." And, whether convert or "born variety," one devotes one's life to the becoming. In your case, you attended Mass faithfully, read Catholic writers from Aquinas to Maritain, corresponded with lay and religious thinkers on theological matters, even made a trip to Lourdes.

You wrote differently from converts, you believed, "the point of view . . . more naturally integrated into the personality." In the same way, I recognize myself to be an essentially Puritan writer, my Catholic perspective an overlay, no less authentic but arguably less "natural" than yours. "I write the way I do because (not though) I am a Catholic," you said, but you deliberately eschewed the Catholic "decor": "Writers like myself who don't use Catholic settings or characters, good or bad, are trying to make it plain that personal loyalty to the person of Christ is imperative, is the structure of man's nature, his necessary direction, etc. The Church, as institution, doesn't come into it one way or another."

When you were twenty-five, you were diagnosed with systemic lupus erythematosus: I, at twenty-nine, with multiple sclerosis. We thus learned early how to dedicate dwindling energies to life's demands. For me, these included marriage, child-rearing, and graduate school. Although I regret none of these undertakings, they did distract me from writing, to which I didn't begin to dedicate myself until I was about the age you were at your death. Fortunately, at diagnosis you were already fully committed to your work. "I have enough energy to write with," you observed, "and as that is all I have any business doing anyhow, I can with one eye squinted take it all as a blessing."

I really believe that you could. You spoke of your work in terms of vocation: "There is a great deal that has to either be given up or be taken away from you if you are going to succeed in writing a body of work. There seem to be other conditions in life that demand celibacy besides the priesthood." Out of context, such a statement might seem sanctimonious, but you exhibited precious little patience with piety. You got on with the life your illness shaped for you: writing every morning; raising peafowl, Chinese geese, and swans; traveling and lecturing when you could. Of the controversial Jesuit Pierre Teilhard de Chardin, from whom you took the story title "Everything That Rises Must Converge," you said, "He was alive to everything there is to be alive to and in the right way." The same could be said of you.

But not of me. Rather, I resemble the suicide of whom you noted, "His tragedy was I suppose that he didn't know what to do with his suffering." I've had the progressive form of MS for over a quarter of a century now, and I'm worn down and out. Less than a month before you died, you sent to an admirer a prayer that begins:

O Raphael, lead us toward those we are waiting for, those
    who are waiting for us:
Raphael, Angel of happy meeting, lead us by the hand
    toward those we are looking for.
May all our movements be guided by your Light and
    transfigured with your joy.

I suppose the prayer is intended for meetings in this world, but I don't see why it has to be. And so I close this letter in the hope that you and I will meet, happily and soon.

        With admiration and affection,
        Nancy

        Nancy Mairs

Three

Teaching Flannery O'Connor

"Some of them need a good stiff dose of Flannery O'Connor"—so I heard my wife Jane say one afternoon after she'd attended a seminar on psychoanalytic theory, to which I belonged as a hospital resident learning to be a psychiatrist. Jane was then a high school teacher of English—had recently discovered O'Connor's fiction and had begun using it in her class in American literature. Now she was urging some medicine on doctors all too sure of themselves as healers, and on me, her husband constantly hearing what she had just taken in—so much said about others in a language heavy with jargon, and not especially modest or at all inclined toward an occasional articulation of self-criticism.

In no time I was reading Flannery O'Connor, to the point that I would recall certain passages from some of her stories (most often, "The Lame Shall Enter First" or "The Artificial Nigger") as I sat at those medical conferences, heard people labeled confidently, called this or that, and described as headed here or there in their future years. We who were learning to "shepherd" others, to be ever so taken with our "heads" as correct monitors of the lives of others, were not being asked to worry about ourselves or about the risks that confront those who stand in authority over others. Thus we are regarded with uncritical acquiescence, if not awe: the secular faiths that are bestowed upon any number of culturally sanctioned seers, among them the social scientists whom a certain Dixie writer observed closely as they went about offering the world their observational expressiveness.

No wonder Flannery O'Connor's stories, and later her essays in *Mystery and Manners*, unnerved me; Mr. Head is, after all, a parent, a teacher of the young. No wonder, at first acquaintance, I began to ask myself what this particular writer's "problem" was, why she insisted on mocking any number of thinking people, ever so literate and well-educated, either literally (as in the way she wrote of "interleckchuls"), or by decided implication in the above mentioned stories and elsewhere. She was, of course, one of those she scorned, so that when one reads her letters (in *The Habit of Being*) one is witness as a deliberately deriding misspelling becomes quite something else: pride confronted, and not only in Manhattan, say, but in Milledgeville.

Ironically, then, Flannery O'Connor has helped some of us who are not unlike her fictional characters and who inhabit a world whose pretenses and smugness she chose not to overlook, but rather, to render with an amused or wry intensity that proves infectious—until, lo and behold, the reader looks inward all too knowingly, worriedly. Again and again, I urge her stories and essays on my students in a college lecture hall, in a medical school classroom, and in the hospital teaching I do. Again and again, too, I am asked about her, about her personal life as well as her body of writing, by young people who have been challenged by her, given pause as well as thought by her—even unnerved by her insistence upon looking squarely at life in all its moral ambiguity, psychological inconsistency. Here, for instance, is a young doctor, headed (if I may) for psychiatry, speaking in a small "discussion group" held in a Boston hospital (1974, a decade after O'Connor's death):

> *You read her, and she won't let go of you! She has you thinking of your real rock-bottom self—who you are and what you believe. That word 'phony' [which] Salinger keeps putting in Holden Caulfield's mouth [in* The Catcher in the Rye*], I kept thinking of it, and I thought to myself: Flannery O'Connor spots the phony everywhere, but she doesn't call it a name, she puts it into a story—she shows it in a character she creates, and she does it [in] so low-key [a manner] that you really get it (I mean she gets you, catches you).*

Days later, as I remembered that class, heard some of the comments made in it courtesy of my tape-recorder, I kept thinking of the word "catcher" in Salinger's novel—because the students felt virtually arraigned and trapped by O'Connor's shrewdly pointed portrayals, to the point that she "got" her readers, "caught" them amidst the flim-flam "rye" of their lives, the self-exaggerations and self-deceptions which they, like so many others, are wont to display. As another student put it in that same seminar: "She's got a laser-beam eye; she misses nothing, and she won't let you pull your usual tricks so you'll overlook what she's spotted!"

Trained in psychiatry and psychoanalysis, I have to sit back in wonder, surprise, amazement, gratitude, great respect, as I hear such words from my students echo my own feelings, my own felt dilemmas, while I struggle to live my life as a teacher, a parent, a guide of the young. Here was a writer of fiction (and non-fiction) who saw through so very much and gave us, unforgettably, what she had come to realize, understand: words on paper that probe far and wide in our American life, that plumb the depths of our social arrangements, of our personal maneuvers of mind and heart, and, not least, of our souls in all their considerable jeopardy amidst their fated time and place on this earthly journey.

Robert Coles

Four

On Visiting Flannery O'Connor's Grave

*This poem, written after a visit to Milledgeville, Georgia
in 1988, is here offered as a tribute to O'Connor on the seventy-
fifth anniversary of her birth.*

Blindingly trite, this calling on the dead,
half obeisance, half an appeasing *there
go I*. We were born in the same year,
her birthday the same day as my favorite brother's,
he too died young of a rare crippling disease. . . .
These self-inflating notions nag me as
I drive through primordial red-clay country
past Brer Rabbit's Pawnshop and Flea Market,
past Uncle Remus's Real Estate and Museum
where I am stuck forever to the Tar Baby
who sticks to the next and next, a circuit
that will carry me by day's end to Memory Hill,

but first, an historic detour just this side
of what the local intelligentsia
in fond self-deprecation call Mudville
to take the cart track up to Andalusia,
the family seat, a serene remove from town,
as in a good Victorian novel.

Here, from the first-floor bedroom window
even on those last dark days, she could see
her beloved peacocks pecking and fanning,
the tribe of philoprogenitive donkeys
ambling down to the farm pond in the meadow,
a grove of ancient pecan trees bending
to be picked. Not antebellum grand,
but commodious Andalusia, with real gardens
harrowed every spring with real manure,
so that it's touching but not surprising that
when Mary McCarthy remarked, years before,
she had come to think of the Eucharist as a symbol,
O'Connor, considerably put out
by lapsed Catholic rhetoric, flared,
"Well, if it's a symbol, to hell with it."

They're haying in the swale. Machinery clatters.
Wood's been cut and stacked. I could walk up
to the empty manse and peer in past a shutter. . . .
The last descendants of O'Connor's critters,
one unkempt little donkey and a hinny—
the casual offspring of a female jennet
and a Shetland stallion—canter across the turf.
They won't come up for carrots, keep
the distance they feel safe in. Fair enough.

In town I pass the college, all mannerly
red brick, held fast as in a spell.
That last-begotten donkey's mournful bray
trails me past dogwood, holly, silver bell. . . .
What can an outsider know, except
the shell of things? The ancestral home
wants painting. Surrounding it, the handsome
latticework brick wall has major gaps.
At the end of the tranquil road, Memory Hill
stands on a rise so slight I want to say
to hell with it. Below the cemetery
mild traffic punctuates crow-call.

Not as I'd pictured her, enthroned
on high, fiercely Promethean
with eagles, say, or lions on the headstone—
but the square, unlandscaped family plot
sans even a drooping willow seems right.
Aligned with her father, three great-aunts opposite,
space for the mother who outlives her yet,
Flannery lies unadorned except by name
who breathed in fire and fed us on the flame.

Maxine Kumin

Five

Revelation

"A Good Man Is Hard to Find" first hit me like a revelation. I was a college student trying to learn to write fiction myself; somehow I had got the idea that a short story should follow a kind of recipe, like a Lady Baltimore cake. Conflict, suspense, resolution; a clear theme; an ending that tied it all up in a neat little bow. Yet when I read that famous last line of "A Good Man Is Hard to Find," I realized that *nothing* was wrapped up here—instead, a whole world opened out before my astonished eyes, a world as wild and scary as life itself. I turned back to the beginning and read it straight through again. I felt like the grandmother in the story, clinging desperately to her outworn beliefs: "I know you're a good man! You're not a bit common! I know you wouldn't shoot a lady! I know you come from good people!" The gun went off in my own head as surely as it went off in those Georgia pines, and a number of my own ideas died instantly along with the grandmother. A story does *not* have to be resolved in the end, I realized. It is enough to glimpse something, momentarily, before it slips back into the dark woods.

Furthermore, a story can be both very funny and deadly serious at the same time. Though she drew a steady bead on salvation and kept it always in her sights, Flannery O'Connor had time for the gross world, too, and for people with all their comic posturing and blundering. The mix of menace and hilarity is evident early on in "A Good Man Is Hard to Find"; the ominous foreshadowing in the lines "this fellow that calls himself The Misfit is aloose from the Federal pen and headed toward Florida and you read here what it says he did to these people" is immediately undercut by the humorous description of the children's mother, "whose face was as broad and innocent as a cabbage and was tied around with a green head-kerchief that had two points on top like rabbit's ears." This kind of juxtaposition continues throughout the story—in the image of Bobby Lee and Hiram ambling back from the woods, for instance, dragging Bobby's ridiculous yellow shirt with blue parrots on it, just after killing him, or in those children screaming, "We've had an accident!" in a frenzy of delight. The world has always struck me as both funny and awful, too, and reading "A Good Man Is Hard to Find" for the first time, I realized that I didn't have to *pick*. What a relief!

The older I get, the more profound this story seems to me. Perhaps the constant presence of death in Flannery O'Connor's life allowed her to see beyond her own years. I never read it now without that deep shock of recognition at the bone, and wonder, and pity for us all.

Lee Smith

Six

Confluence

F lannery O'Connor is a writer who has
affected me in a way that is difficult to
articulate. It's hard to fully honor the complexity of the influence I imagine she has had on me as a writer, but recently I
experienced a certain fortuity involving a Flannery O'Connor
story that perhaps exemplifies something about the kinship I
feel with her work.

One evening I felt a sudden yen to reread her story "The
Turkey." Maybe this is owing to the fact that my blue-
crowned conure had been droopy of late, victim of a stressful
molt, and so I thought I'd be encouraged by the resolve that
characterizes the wounded bird in the beginning of that
story (despite its ultimate demise); or maybe it is that I have
always found turkeys (maligned though they often are) to be
somehow automatically poignant, enchanting even, and I
was just in need of sonic bird ju-ju. Unlike O'Connor, I am
guilty of gussying up the plights of animals, particularly

those of birds, with a romantic and therefore anthropomorphized sheen, self-possessed and plumed in courage as I imagine them to be. I have that magical realist tendency to invest the lives of animals with all sorts of mystical significance, which, if observed with a discerning enough eye, stands to heal whatever ails the hampered human, and so when in need of magic, I rarely let harsh realities get in my way.

A few days after rereading this story, I went to see a film I'd not seen since its original release in 1989, Emir Kustarica's *Time of the Gypsies*. I had completely forgotten how prominently a spellbound turkey figures in this film, and I felt a vague charge kindle the skin of my arms as I took in the coincidence and watched the turkey slowly open its wings to the extra-sensory vibration its owner aimed at it with thick-spectacled magnetism. I was as thoroughly crushed as Perhan, the spoon-levitating gypsy boy who was training the turkey to rise to an invisible influence, when this turkey met its end in a soup pot.

The minor coincidence, which no doubt seems perfectly insignificant to anyone less inclined to see turkeys as swollen with pathos as I am, would have been quickly forgotten had it not been for what happened the next morning. On my way into town, I had to slow down as a gaggle of Canadian geese ambled across the road. I've had plenty of truck with city geese and know they do not trouble themselves too much with the impatience of mere motorists, so it didn't surprise me particularly when they didn't flee at my approach, but what did surprise me was the realization that these were not geese at all—these were in fact wild turkeys, a whole flock of them, crossing the road! I grew up in Kansas City, Kansas, where I was often stalled by the meanderings of all manner of farm animals, but never had I been halted by a flock of wild turkeys trekking across a street in my own neighborhood. I felt so charmed I could hardly accelerate.

I have always identified with the boy in the Flannery O'Connor story who worries his father by playing too much by himself and who curses himself silly in the face of a disappointment and failure that threatens to corroborate the doubts he knows his family has about him. After he has let loose with all the oaths he can think of, Ruller imagines fibbing to his parents and asks, "What difference would it make? Yeah, God, what difference would it make?" This blasphemous thought startles him a little, but then he gives himself over to a sense of himself as an outlaw in his own family, as though he were trying to taunt God out of hiding. He's miffed at God for having teased him with the promise of catching a turkey, thereby earning him the notoriety of being "an unusual boy," only to snatch the distinction away from him. Again, he chides himself for such thinking, just before he stumbles upon the turkey, there lying dead before him. Ruller reads this as a moment of grace, imagines that this lifeless turkey is evidence that he's been chosen by God for some special purpose, sees favorable portent in the happy fortuity of those "blood-soaked" feathers.

Like Ruller, I sometimes heckle God, the cosmos, to see what will fall at my feet. I am vulnerable to what some would call magical thinking and cannot help seeing significance in small confluences. Like O'Connor, I have an abiding respect for mystery and prefer that possibility remain just that, prefer that it not get roped at the ankles. And I have come to understand, as Ruller does, that moments of grace, whether genuine or manufactured, cannot be sustained for long. My own characters frequently transcend, in one way or another, their circumstances, and this leads them momentarily to imagine they can reverse that old dialectic, can breach the divide and skin themselves, coax the flesh toward spirit. But they're flesh in the end and have to reckon with the melancholy that accompanies this limitation.

These events become significant only because I choose to notice them and constellate them in a way that is meaningful to me. This is what fiction writers do, impose order on experience, and I try to do so in a way that is respectful of the unexpected, the unempirical, the mysterious. In the work of Flannery O'Connor, grace, magic, mystery, revelation all tend to be held in check in the end by a hard-bargaining, Old Testament-style accounting. Ruller loses his booty, The Misfit kills the grandmother at the very moment of her self-lessness, Mrs. Turpin awakens to the notion she'll be pulling up the rear when it comes time to file into heaven. (And I understand that some of those carousing turkeys that transported me are likely by now to have met a Thanksgiving fate.) In my own work, the price is not always so high, but flashes of instructive mystery are fleeting, revelations invariably fall short—always a frustration, the frustration of the flesh yearning to exceed itself. My experience and those of my characters are not unlike Ruller's in that the bottom often drops out of moments of grace, and they give way to a feeling of being dogged at the heels by "Something Awful," yet this only serves to heighten my appreciation for and sensitivity to them, the fact that they're consequential. I don't know that Flannery O'Connor's fiction has helped me to understand this so much as it has given me license to examine and try to word what this means, and because that's what I spend some of my most enjoyable days doing, I'm grateful for that.

Kellie Wells

Seven

Vertigo

The first time I read anything by Flannery O'Connor must have been in the mid 1950s. I remember purchasing on the same lucky day *A Good Man Is Hard to Find* and Shirley Ann Grau's *The Black Prince and Other Stories*. I admired both books and read them slowly, prolonging the experiences.

I discovered, though, that I didn't exactly enjoy O'Connor's stories, at least not in the same way that I enjoyed Grau's. I felt then what I still feel when I reread some of the more striking of them. The sensation is less intense, after so prolonged an exposure, but I would still describe it as a sort of vertigo. I still seem utterly displaced, *unplaced,* upon finishing "A Good Man Is Hard to Find" or "The Artificial Nigger" or "Good Country People" or "Revelation" or any of nine or ten others.

It is not that I am dismayed or baffled by her characters. Indeed, I find them all too familiar. I grew up among poor whites, some of whom could be as treacherous, hypocritical, willfully ignorant, and downright mean as in any portrait O'Connor furnishes. I knew more than one Appalachian male who would declare his ardent hatred for "niggers" without ever having met an African American in the flesh. I can still recall the happily contemptuous snarl of one individual when he framed his sentence: "All them goddam niggers ought to be hung by the balls."

Nor did I doubt that these types could and should be limned in literature. I admired then, and still admire, the crackingly energetic stories of Erskine Caldwell, who stamped his imprimatur upon these character types with an almost savage forcefulness.

But with Caldwell I knew where I was supposed to stand. The angry writer is a warm writer, and it was obvious that Caldwell's heart was stoked by righteous fires. (Someone once called him "God's Little Acher.") With O'Connor I didn't know where to place my sympathies. I knew where not to—but that is a different matter. Critics have made agile arguments on behalf of her Misfit, but I can find him no more than a murderous halfwit with vague pretensions to intellection. When he makes his famous statement at the end of "A Good Man," I am more puzzled than moved: "Shut up, Bobby Lee. It's no real pleasure in life."

I read Baudelaire unstintingly and Barbey d'Aurevilly and Georges Bataille and the dark Mark Twain and Shakespeare's *Troilus* and Poe—ever more fervently, Poe. But these masters of the sardonic fade in comparison to the tone that Flannery O'Connor strikes in my mind. At first I thought to describe her dominant attitude toward her figures and their situations as "disgust" but found the term too warm. To be disgusted is to be repelled, of course, but for me the word implies an unwilling distaste; disgusted, one is repelled in spite of himself.

O'Connor is cooler than that; she is subzero. Icy disdain pervades her pages, and she is as religiously pitiless as Virgil admonishes Dante to become as he guides the trembling poet through the horrors of the Inferno. But O'Connor's intensity of presentation—that phalanx of tartly precise detail, that perfect-pitch reporting of dialogue—strikes a new note. Some of the naturalist writers—Zola, Huysmans, Norris—gave us case studies instead of characters; they didn't so much present situations as rub our noses in them. O'Connor goes these writers one better by giving us *exempla*, figures that illustrate the results of a broken covenant. They are almost medieval in their emblematic aspect, can seem to have stepped off the walls of any hell scene in a thirteenth-century cathedral chapel in Siena.

They are just as effective as these figures, too. O'Connor was a favorite with a certain type of graduate creative writing student I taught in the 1970s. Privately, I dubbed this crew "the motorless bikers." Though they could not afford the machines, they often wore biker regalia, talked chopshop, and rocked their legs and butts with the old Brando swagger. I would have thought "Kerouac," but it was O'Connor that shone in their imaginations, and on one enlightening occasion I noticed that one of them had decorated the back of his black leather jacket with The Misfit's motto: "It's no real pleasure in life."

The joke doesn't get any more comically bitter than that, I suppose. These brash lads, avid for literature, greedy for attention, had made themselves into figures that their beloved author might have used in one of her stories, shining upon their callow and confused aspirations that clinical arc

lamp that revealed every mole, wart, and pimple in any coun-
tenance. They would have withered under her gaze like sun-
baked earthworms, but the experience would have done
them more than a mite of good.

There are some writers I can read only in long stretches—
Thomas Wolfe, for example, and Thomas Mann—and others
of whom I partake only a little at a time, one or two chapters,
or two short stories at most. Kafka is one of these and
Tommaso Landolfi and Borges and Sade. Chief among them
is Flannery O'Connor. A fifty-page read is overwhelming;
sixty pages are numbing. I could not read 100 pages of her
work any more than I could listen for three solid hours to the
music of Anton Webern. I would become dizzy and a little
nauseated, and I would begin to grip too tightly the arms of
my chair.

Great stuff.

Dangerous stuff.

Fred Chappell

Eight

Last Encounter with the Enemy

The boy knew her name, all right, but he liked to call her the peacock lady. Ever since that article in the Sunday supplement, with the photographs of her propped on crutches surrounded by peachickens pecking the dirt and her scowling hard as if she knew the callow young newspaper photographer was the devil himself and she wasn't fooled for a minute, the boy had thought of her that way. After he'd scampered off the Greyhound from Atlanta and found a taxi, he'd thought maybe even the illiterates in this godforsaken town might have heard of her, since she was famous and all their own, so he'd spoken her name to the driver and asked if he knew where she lived. But the driver, a dumb kid with Elvis sideburns, just wrinkled his nose and said, "Huh? You ain't got the *ad*dress?" So the boy had prompted him, "You know, dontcha? The famous lady writer? The peacock lady?" That last phrase had done it. Elvis smirked and said yup, he'd driven a couple of priests out there last week and the damn peahens had been stalking around all over the place—yeah, he remembered—and he'd rapped the meter and off they went.

The boy had sat back, mightily pleased.

By the time the cab slowed along the Eatonton highway, he'd gotten so deeply enmeshed in a fantasy scenario of what lay ahead that he hadn't understood the big moment was here. He'd read everything the woman had written, but because he was a puny little towhead fatally underestimated by adults the peacock lady wouldn't guess at that. He planned to make an impression by casually dropping things into the conversation that would amaze her. Soon enough she would realize he was her equal if not better; and then, being a woman, she would probably start confiding in him. Though he was only eleven and small for his age, maybe she'd develop a crush on him, a little. Unmarried women were prone to that, he'd heard. He knew what probably lay underneath that exterior of the nun-like spectacles she wore, and the fearsome scowl; he wasn't fooled by the black going-to-church dress and string of pearls, or by the smart-alecky comments she made in interviews about "modern man" whenever she got off on one of her tangents about the Holy Apostolic Church and all the rest. He supposed she'd be vulnerable enough to a modern man if a real live one strolled right into her kitchen.

As for the Church, he went to parochial school, and his careful references to the nuns, especially his English teacher Sister Imelda for whom he was writing his extra-credit essay on the peacock lady's work, were probably the reason she'd agreed to see him. He'd tossed in a whopper about being an altar boy, too, but he'd long ago repudiated all that nonsense. At some point he'd spring on her the essay's brilliant first sentence that had come to him only yesterday: "Life itself is the peacock lady's wound, and the Church is her band-aid." He'd written down the line and read it over maybe three hundred times and thought it was about the cleverest thing he'd done yet. He couldn't wait to see the look on her face.

The driver stopped the cab beside the road and jerked around. "You wanna get out here, or you want me to pull on up that driveway?"

The boy squinted toward the white clapboard house, maybe a quarter-mile down a rutted lane, and then to the dark ridge of trees he recognized at once from the fiction. It had rained yesterday and the lane was muddy, full of potholes with standing reddish-brown water. He supposed Elvis was worried about his shiny hubcaps.

"If I'd wanted to walk, I don't reckon I'd have hired a taxi, now would I?" the boy said.

His heart pounded queerly in his excitement. For two or three years he had been scribbling odd little stories in his school notebooks, and he'd started typing them up and giving them to Sister Imelda, who would read them aloud to the class. "It seems we have an aspiring *writer* in our midst," she said the first time, a comment that had made him squirm with pleasure, and he didn't care that later he got shoved around at recess for sucking up to the teacher. His stories were about people drowning in floods and people kidnapped and tortured by ruthless thugs and babies born with such horrible deformities that their mothers plotted to kill them, but none of this fazed Sister Imelda, who said the boy had "a real flair for language." So when he'd read the Sunday supplement article about the peacock lady he'd gotten very excited that there was somebody else who not only wrote odd things, but got paid for them and got her picture in the paper; he'd read the article countless times and knew it was only a matter of time before they would meet.

Then he'd read her stories, which he thought were pretty good (he knew his were better), and he'd gone to the school library and let old Sister Blanche look up things other people wrote about the peacock lady, and some interviews she'd given; that's when his stomach had begun to turn. All that palaver about the Church. The Church this, the Church that. He was disappointed, but guessed he shouldn't have been surprised. A lady writer, after all. Probably would have joined the convent if she hadn't lucked into publishing a book.

As they pulled in sight of the screened-in porch, he caught a glimpse of her inside, waiting, in one of those ordinary metal porch chairs; the aluminum crutches were propped against a second, empty chair, and a third had been placed opposite the woman, across from a rickety old table. All this for him, he thought. He pulled out his billfold and gave the driver one of the tens he'd been lifting these past few days from his mother's purse—he could always go to confession, he'd thought, smirking—and strode forthrightly toward the back door, which stood propped open to the cool spring morning with a gigantic milk can.

"Come back in two hours," he spat over his shoulder at Elvis. "And don't be late."

The peacock lady had turned in her chair and was smiling as he climbed the brick steps and entered the porch. "Hello there," she said. "You must be—"

"Nice to meetcha!" the boy cried, rushing forward, "I been looking forward to this all week long!"

He pumped her hand, noticing how white and pasty her upper arm looked in the sleeveless black dress. His heart glowed with pride. It was the same dress she'd worn for the Atlanta paper that day they came to take her picture! He'd debated whether to dress up or not and now was glad he'd picked the long navy pants he wore on Sundays when his mother dragged him to mass and the white Ban-Lon shirt an aunt had sent for his birthday. He'd thought even a lady writer might have appreciated his usual T-shirt and cut-offs, taking him for a youthful bohemian, but then he'd worried she might think that was improper for a meeting of two intellectuals and had opted for attire befitting a serious occasion.

"Glad you could come," she said, with her measured smile. He saw how intently her blue eyes fixed on him, behind those chunky-looking glasses. He looked down, his gaze settling on the nicked wooden table that was stacked with books surrounding a glass-covered cake dish piled high with little white cookies. The powdered sugary disks made his mouth water instantly. The woman added, "Have a seat."

As he took the chair, pausing first over the books and nodding as if he were intimately familiar with each volume and glancing sideways at the pile of cookies, the woman kept giving him the same careful smile. When she'd first seen him emerge from the taxi, she'd worried for a moment about keeping a straight face. She knew she was dealing with a schoolboy—that was part of the reason she'd agreed to see him, though she tired easily these days and didn't welcome visitors so readily as she once did—but she'd expected a tall gangly high school boy, not this little blond child who looked as if he'd made his first communion week before last. The letter he'd sent had been semi-literate, but she'd ascribed that to ignorance rather than extreme youth, and now she was glad indeed that she'd invited him down. She wished her mother hadn't gone into town for the afternoon; lately, Regina spoke the word "interviewers" in the same tone an old countryman might say "revenuers" and liked to disappear when one was coming out. But she'd have gotten a kick out of this.

"Your mama let you come all this way by yourself?" she said kindly, but at once the boy frowned as if the question offended him.

"I come on my own," he said cryptically, looking off. "It's Sareday, you know. I ain't got no school."

Maybe it's just as well, if that's how they teach you to speak, the woman thought, but she kept her smile going.

"She knows you're here, don't she?"

She had a bad habit of adopting the grammar of her interlocutor, whether a visiting theologian or a white trash dairyman, but it was a habit she hadn't tried very hard to break. Somehow she felt it helped in her writing.

"I come on my own," the boy repeated, stubbornly. He reached into his pants pocket and pulled out a tiny spiral notebook with a cheap fountain pen clipped to its cover; she'd already noted, approvingly, the boy's ink-splotched fingers. He added, "Like I said, it's nice to meet you and all. I reckon we can get started, if it's all right by you."

She bent forward and set aside the glass top of the cake dish. "Would you care for some of these cookies? I'd planned to give you chocolate chip, but we're out. My mother's at the store right now."

The boy reached out for one of the wedding cookies—she saw that his hand was shaking—and popped it into his mouth. "That's OK, my mama buys these too," he said. "I like them all right."

"I'd fetch you some sweet tea, but you'd probably get it quicker if you went in the kitchen yourself." She glanced toward the crutches.

The boy shook his head. "Nope, ain't thirsty," he said. "Had me a Coke on the bus."

She sat back, already feeling a little tired. But this was certainly an interesting specimen. Last week it had been a couple of Jesuits who'd droned for more than two hours about doctrinal niceties she considered about as important as hen droppings, and a few days before that a pop-eyed woman historical novelist who sold more books in one day than she'd sold in her whole life, but who'd come to "pay her respects" and get an "expert opinion" on character development. The woman had said she was tired of writing historical bestsellers and wanted to write what was in her heart, and when the expert opined that if characters didn't develop on their own there wasn't much you could do for them and anyway that what was in her heart probably would be much less interesting to most people then lively, made-up history, the woman had left in a huff. That visit was shorter yet had made her more tired than her strenuous afternoon with the Jesuits.

But this child sitting here, his legs crossed at the ankles and swinging about a foot above the porch floor, was something else altogether.

"All right then," she said, in what she hoped was an encouraging voice, "I reckon whatever you aim to ask, you can ask." Hoping to break the ice a little, she added, "Just don't ask me about none of my boyfriends, now."

At that the boy's eyes—a pretty but veiled soft blue—met hers directly. He even gave a little smile. "I wasn't gonna ask you nothing personal," he said.

She laughed out loud. "That's good," she told him. "Then shoot."

For a few minutes he lobbed the usual questions at her, and she batted the memorized answers back. To her surprise the boy kept flipping open the little notebook, which was filled with page after page of his large, left-slanting, childish handwriting. He'd written all the questions out! Lately she'd come to believe that no one could surprise her anymore, but just when you dared think your wisdom was complete, along came a new twist in human nature you couldn't have anticipated. Several of the questions she recognized from recent interviews she'd given and it occurred to her that a little speech about plagiarism might be in order, but each time she looked into his fresh pink-cheeked face and virginal blue eyes, she had to remember how young this child was, for all his prematurely mannish, even old-mannish pride. Now he asked a question that was so ridiculous—"Please give me your observation on the issue of point of view in today's fiction"—that again she laughed aloud.

"Come on, boy, ain't you thought up any better questions than that?"

He met her smile with a challenging look. "There's some says you got a problem with thisyer point of view," he observed.

She gazed out into the yard, where one of the hens had paused to regard herself in a rain puddle.

"That may be, but I've got bigger problems than that," she said.

He kept staring.

"All right," she relented, "the fact is, you're not supposed to switch it around while you're telling a story, but I do it all the time."

Though the boy supposed this was an evasive answer, he decided to let it pass. Everything was going according to plan; he was just biding his time while she warmed to him. One of the newspapers had suggested that she was "defensive" about her work and so he thought a few routine, boring questions for which she had pat answers would help catch her off guard. He glanced at his Timex and saw that half an hour had passed; he guessed it was time to turn up the pressure. He rubbed one forearm across his brow, for the late-morning sun had shifted and he now sat bisected by a plane of light that had warmed him uncomfortably even though this was March and the air wafting inside from the propped-open door was cool. Already he'd scooted his chair as far into the shade as he could, but the sun kept sliding sideways upon him, implacably, while the peacock lady sat comfortably in her patch of shade, observing him. He thought to change his mind about the iced tea but decided that would show weakness so he plunged ahead, flipping another page in his notebook.

"Okay, religion," he said, as if ticking items off a list. "What is the religious sig—sig—" Damn, he couldn't read his own words he'd copied from one of Sister Blanche's articles.

"Significance?" the peacock lady said.

"—of yer stories!" he shouted.

She sat quietly for a moment. An almost melancholy look came over her face.

"That's a tall order," she pointed out.

He smiled; when they got sad, it was time for you to turn on the charm.

"Well, I didn't come here to ask you no silly questions," he said.

Her answer came quick. "Son, I really can't figure out why you did come here. This seems like a mighty big project for somebody your age. They assign things like this in parochial school these days?" Behind the thick glasses her eyes seemed to narrow. "By the way, you ain't told me your name. You didn't even sign that letter you sent me."

He tried not to smile too broadly; she'd fallen right into his trap. He gazed off through the screen enclosing them to the woods, uncomfortably aware of the line of sweat along his upper lip. It had even collected on his eyelids. Out in the yard a couple of the peachickens were indulging in a grooming ritual, and on the opposite side of a fence in the middle distance a few cows stood picturesquely, their tails swishing. One of the peacocks sat sunning himself on a fencepost, his long tail feathers almost reaching the ground. Beyond the fence loomed the dark woods, and he thought about everything that was going on out there, the dead bodies oozing blood and the kids against trees getting beaten within an inch of their lives and the strange violations so dark and perverted even *he* couldn't imagine them. Maybe if there was time before Elvis came back he'd take a stroll through the pines and have a peek at the blood and the mayhem.

"Well?" she asked, adjusting her glasses. He caught her checking her watch, just a flick of her pasty-white wrist. "What's your name, boy?"

He looked her full in the face. "I'm Jesus," he said.

She did a good job of hiding her shock, he'd give her that; a couple of faint lines scored her forehead but that was all. "Is that a fact? Are you part Mexican, child? You sure don't look it."

"No m'am, I'm Swedish on my daddy's side—he's dead and you don't want to ast where is he now—and my mama's folks came from over in Switzerland. But that ain't got nothing to do with who *I* am."

"Is that a fact?" the peacock lady said. She looked pleased, but whether pleased with him or herself he couldn't quite tell. Her lips had flattened in an amused little smile. "I guess it's a relief, Jesus," she said, "to know that you're a Catholic."

Another trap. For the second time he reached across and grabbed one of the sugary white cookies. He longed for something to drink, for now he was bathed in sunlight except for his right elbow and the cookie was stale and dry. He chewed rapidly, hacking up the spit to swallow it down.

"Just because I go to school where they's penguin teachers don't mean I'm Cathlick," he said. "My mama's Church of God and I'm the same. We believe the Church of Rome is an out-and-out fraud and that the pope aims to take over the govvermint!"

All this was a lie—of course his mother was Catholic, and until he wised up he'd been one, too—but he wanted to erase that little smile off the woman's face.

"You sure have lots of opinions for a youngster!" the peacock lady said. She leaned forward, her dark eyes enlarged behind the glasses. "Now why don't you tell me? Who are you, really?"

"I believe I'm the one s'post to be asking things, but I'll answer you. I reckon I'm a temple of the Holy Ghost," he said, narrowing his eyes as he checked her reaction, "and I'm that good man you think's so hard to find, and I'm sure enough good country people, too! So put that in your pipe and smoke it."

Her eyes blazed, but with pleasure rather than anger. She stayed bent forward, as if daring him to peek down her dress. But the neck was too high, and the old-lady pearls were in the way.

"That's a heap of erudition you just displayed," she said. "I'm mighty impressed."

He'd practiced the line for weeks and was proud of himself for getting it out; sometimes, practicing, he'd stumbled a little. He should know better than to doubt himself.

"I thank you," he said.

"But really, Jesus, I wish you'd tell me what I did to deserve an audience this morning."

He jerked his head around, supposing a crowd had gathered behind him, but then he understood; she'd meant that *he* was the audience. He'd worried all week that she might start talking over his head, which she could probably do just because she'd read a lot of books he knew better than to bother with, so he decided to cut her off at the pass by changing the subject.

"I got my reasons," he said, "but you listen to this. Now s'pose I told you that on the one hand, I'm eleven years old and I go to this school where the penguin ladies teach, and I write down little stories that would make your glasses flip backwards if you read them. But on the other hand, I'm something else again. Okay, I ain't Jesus, I just said that to get your attention. But I'll tell you what I really am—a *prophet*."

He folded his arms and waited for that to impress her. She was cagey, all right, but his words had set her back in her chair. She grasped its metal arms as tightly as she would have gripped her crutches.

"A prophet!" she marveled.

He couldn't tell if she was ridiculing him but decided it didn't matter. He'd get the last laugh. He continued in a solemn voice, as if she hadn't spoken: "Had my first vision come along last weekend—hit me right between the eyes just like a bullet. The future done come to me in a blaze of light and glory, and this is what I seen. Now picture this: it ain't 1964 no more. Nope, and it ain't 1970, and not 1980, neither. Why, it ain't even this dang century any more!" He paused a beat, just for the effect. "No ma'am, it's the year *two thousand!* And guess what: you're dead as a doornail and I'm all growed up and somebody done ast me to write down something about *you!*"

The peacock lady's gaze had drifted off, not as if she were troubled by this outlandish scenario but as if it bored her. She said, "If you agreed to such a thing, you'd be mighty hard up for writing assignments."

The boy smiled grimly. From inside the house, a door slammed. She looked aside, briefly. "That must be Louise . . ." she murmured.

The boy's heart leapt: what an opportunity. She was a tough nut to crack, but this ought to split the shell wide open.

He leaned forward and said, with a little flutter of his eyelids, "Or maybe it's Parker. Maybe Parker's back."

That got her attention; she straightened abruptly and no longer pretended to smile.

"All right, boy, this was fun, but I get tired awful easily these days. Now that story about Parker ain't been printed yet, and there's only five or six people in America who've read it. Who put you up to this? Was it Betty? Was it Cecil?"

The boy made his eyes round and puzzled. "Betty who? Cecil who?" he said innocently.

"You didn't come here for any school assignment, child. Now who are you? I'm all tired out and I don't have time to waste."

He was feeling overheated, but he stood and held his pen aloft as though displaying a sacred relic. "I told you, I'm a prophet, and I come with a pen instead of a sword. I'm here from the next century to tell you that God is dead and so are you!"

She gave him a stony look. "If He was dead, then I might as well be."

"And as for these stories of yourn, they done been ana-
lyzed, psychologized, feminized, disconstructed, put in their
historical *con*test, and hung on out to dry!"

"And one more thing," the boy said impatiently, tired of
her stalling. This might have been the moment to lay that
brilliant sentence from his essay on her: *Life itself is the peacock
lady's wound....* But no, there was no time for that. Instead he
shouted: "Ain't nobody believes that God claptrap but you!"

From behind, as he struggled to his feet and stood tri-
umphant against her steely glare, he could hear the cries of
those stupid peachickens. He glanced around and saw a couple of gray females regarding him from the lane, and from
another direction several males dragged their long tails out
of the flowerbeds (dollops of bedraggled chrysanthemums,
roses) alongside the house. Some fluttered down from the
roof, while others scurried out from the crepe myrtle. He
glanced around and saw more descending from the oaks and
cedars, from the fig trees.

The peacock lady bent forward in her chair, her eyes nar-
rowed to slits.

"You're mighty young to be so—so hard," she said, almost
as if talking to herself and not to him. "But not too old to be
saved, that's for sure."

He slapped his knee and let out a loud guffaw. "Lady, your
head must be hard as a rock!" he cried. He demonstrated by
knocking a fist against his own head, then he reached down in
a cavalier gesture and swiped another little white cookie off
the plate. As soon as he popped it inside his mouth, he knew
his error. His mouth was dry as sand, and now the chalky mess
of cookie and powdered sugar kept expanding the more he
chewed, like a fistful of ashes he could neither swallow nor spit
out. His very throat seemed paralyzed.

"You got something more you want to say, boy?" the woman asked. She reached for her crutches, deciding she'd had enough. This poor deluded child had angered her, yes, and she had no idea who'd told him about "Parker's Back," which she'd been writing and rewriting for several years and wasn't done with yet; but entertaining infantile blasphemy hadn't been part of her plans this morning. After all, shortly before this boy arrived she'd gotten home from a ten o'clock funeral—one of Regina's old friends—and hanging there on her crutches at the cemetery while the minister droned his consolations, she'd wondered how soon she'd be returning here. In a horizontal position, most likely. After she and Regina drove home in silence, she'd been too tired even to change her clothes, and now here was this maddening child sent to try her patience. Sent as a joke, she supposed, but it wasn't funny any more.

Struggling with the crutches, she got to her feet, watching as the boy clutched at his throat, his eyes locked onto hers in an outraged, pleading look.

She said gently, "Just turn around, boy. Believe. God is watching you—in the present and in the future, too. Anyone can be a prophet, son. Anyone can live forever. Just turn around and behold the Lord!"

His face was turning blue, a few shades darker than his eyes, but he turned as if helpless to do anything but obey. Just outside the opened screen door the peacocks were approaching the brick steps, their cawing sound risen now to a chorus of screams: *Eee-Ooo-ii! Eee-ooo-ii!* Gathering close, the hens in front and the cocks arrayed behind them, the birds resembled an audience of outraged, elderly citizens prepared to tell the boy just what they thought of his pretensions. As though following some divine choreography, the peacocks had begun strutting forward and back, heads pecking the air, their blue necks and crested heads jerking in majestic spasms, their screams growing louder and more urgent as the seconds passed. The boy, gripping his throat, writhed on his feet as though performing some doomed parody of the peacocks' dance. The birds shrieked so that even her own ears hurt: *Eee-ooo-ii! Eee-ooo-ii!* Their distinctively sour, peppery scent wafted inside the porch on the morning air. And now, as if obeying a summons, all the birds went silent and the peacocks in rustling grandeur lifted and spread their tails—each a shimmering aureole of bright blue-green and bronze, each tipped with a tiny sunlike burst of light.

She pointed with one of her crutches. "Observe and fall to your knees, boy! You are face to face with God's revelation! Don't dare to deny him! Don't dare to turn away!"

The boy glanced back at her, his face a swollen bruised purple, his mouth stubbornly clamped shut. He glared as if to say that he would die refusing to accept her obscene visions, he would stand here as a prophet of unbelief and a martyr to the future! Soon enough she would be dead, and he'd have the last word and the last goddamn laugh! She read all this in his desperate squinted eyes, while the majestic peacocks circled the porch in their full, brilliant display, which after all these years could still rend her heart.

She lifted one of her crutches and slammed it with all her might against the side of the boy's head. Then, aiming carefully with the other crutch, she struck him across the back, observing with satisfaction the mass of whitish glop shooting from his mouth just as he stumbled down the steps and fell into the grass. The chickens went running. The peacocks' tails descended quickly as they rushed off, their wild screams lowering to ordinary squeaks and squabbles.

Exhausted, she dragged herself to the edge of the porch and observed him lying there in the yard, his little hands fallen from his throat, the flushed pink of innocence returning to his cheeks. His eyes were open and blinking but emptied of all that rage, all that horror.

He stared up at her, wondering.

"Vengeance is mine, saith the Lord," she allowed herself with an angry smile.

She turned and hobbled back inside the house.

He couldn't remember much about Elvis helping him inside the car or the ride back to the station. Numbed as though stumbling through a dream, he found a seat at the back of the bus. He spoke to no one and no one spoke to him. Half an hour later, he sat with his head leaned back against the seat and watched as the desiccated fields, still beaten down by winter, streamed along his window in a colorless blur. Eventually his gaze fell to his lap, and he understood that he held something between his folded hands—it was a single, brightly colored feather, a thing of such singular beauty and perfection that it seemed to match this new, shy, peaceful emotion inside him, something not of this earth.

He kept holding and staring at the feather, all the way home.

Greg Johnson

Nine

The Goddess of a Secular Church

To say that Flannery O'Connor made you want to be a writer, either by herself or in a constellation of others, looks presumptuous, opening as it does the debate as to whether one *is* a writer, etc. But let us forego the niceties of vanity and the invidiousness of comparison in the confession. Let us say that coming upon Flannery O'Connor at a young and thinking-about-it age would be like coming across Janis Joplin if you were young and thinking about being a rock singer. You see before you a model of someone utterly mad with passion and consumed by a vision and desperate to execute it. And you see a considerable technician. It is not an exaggeration to say you see someone driven and holy, a goddess of her church.

I have seen even the fool who would not be a writer fall under the thrall of Flannery O'Connor. When I was flunking out of graduate chemistry school at the University of Tennessee in 1975, a fellow who was not flunking out—who would become a radio chemist—discovered her and began putting quotes from her work up on the wall. Scientists like to put ironic things up on the wall, I have noticed, perhaps more than other people like to. Or perhaps it is safer to say that scientists put up on the wall that which is actually funny as opposed to that which is supposed to be funny. I remember Bill Rogers at Tennessee putting a page from "Good Country People" up on our suite door; on it he had highlighted:

> *Here she went about all day in a six-year-old skirt and a yellow sweatshirt with a faded cowboy on a horse embossed on it.*

That Hulga, *née* Joy, who had a Ph.D. in philosophy—he was getting his in chemistry—wore a shirt with a cowboy on it delighted Bill Rogers. It was a perfect note of insouciance, and perfectly put. I suspect he appreciated the writing of it as well—that the cowboy was on a horse (incomplete to have one on the ground), that the cowboy was faded (any cowboy in a storm), that it was a sweatshirt (a lower-class garment), that the sweatshirt was yellow (ditto: tacky and loud), that the image was *embossed* (a precision that said *yes!*)—but we did not discuss the details of O'Connor's perfect nuancing.

It had, I think, already obtained there in our suite that I would be a casualty of chemistry. I had failed all the placement tests and was in impossibly broad remedial survey courses; Bill Rogers had placed out and was properly moving on to the kind of work graduate school was about. It must have escaped that I was looking for relief along the lines of something like what O'Connor had been up to. Bill's posting of the good stuff she could do—it is possible I put him onto her—contained, I think, an implicit set of questions from him to me:

"Okay, if I go on to nuke the world, and you do this, will you do it this well? Can you be this outrageous and this technically deft? Can you nuke them as she nukes them? We will not exclude you from the club of clear thinkers here if you can do this. . . ."

My immediate answer to Bill Rogers was to check out the entire *oeuvre* of Tennessee Williams and read it at night instead of Morrison and Boyd, the deans of organic chemistry, and in three months I was on the street. Bill and I had each bought an Army field-hospital tent, thinking clearly that for twenty dollars so much canvas alone could not be had, let alone configured in a tent the size of a small house, and I put mine in the trunk of my Nova and headed for Houston, at one end of Williams' Chef Menteur/Old Spanish Trail, and Bill put his in his apartment and headed for the Oak Ridge nuclear reactors. Thinking clearly, the last thing I did in Knoxville was climb on a roof and run a screeching A/C compressor through with a broom handle. I was O'Connor's heathen, raging secularly.

Ten years or so later Bill Rogers, from the purview of a nuclear reactor in Alabama, would write me that I had entered "Southern writerhood," and now I am to say something about that relevant to Flannery O'Connor. She is a writer for this writer for these reasons:

She wrote of Teilhard de Chardin and of chickens. "I got me X peahens." ("Why do your characters wear hats?" "To keep their heads warm.") From her cool remove of faith she could interpolate the hot, warped psyche in people for whom believing in Jesus is a matter of life and death. As goddesses are supposed to, she held a high-minded station from which she could be a low-minded interlocutor among mortals. As she wrote in a letter to "A" in 1960, "As a fiction writer, I am interested first in Enoch as Enoch and Haze as Haze. Haze is repulsed by the shriveled man he sees merely because it is hideous. He has a picture of his new jesus—shriveled as it is. Therefore it certainly does have meaning for Haze. Why would he throw it away if it didn't? Its meaning is in its rejection. Haze, even though a primitive, is full of the poison of the modern world. That is in part responsible for some of the comic effect."

What is finally enduring about O'Connor's allure has to do, I think, with what I have come to call the outrageousness quotient (plausibility of telling over implausibility of event). Or, to be more precise, the grandmother who reads the newspaper article about The Misfit and selfishly counsels her family to go the other way is killed by The Misfit. No one quarrels. The bull who chews Mrs. May's hedge, wearing from it a crown of thorns, in the first paragraph, gores Mrs. May in the penultimate paragraph. To applause. Hulga's mother sees the country boy as the eponymous "good country people" and "the salt of the earth." After he has put her daughter's wooden leg in his valise with his whiskey and prophylactic, she says, "Why, that looks like that nice dull young man that tried to sell me a Bible yesterday," adding, "He was so simple . . . but I guess the world would be better off if we were all that simple." He has stolen the leg.

Flannery O'Connor is a writer who can get away with anything. She is like Kafka in this regard, closer to Kafka than any other American writer. How is it done? O'Connor supplies the answer in a neat formula in a letter to John Hawkes in 1950, "The more fantastic the action the more precise the writing and this is the way it ought to be." How do you render plausible the implausibility of so simple a leg-stealing

Bible salesman? The kernel of the answer is in precision like this:

> *Smiling, he lifted his hat which was new and wide-brimmed. He had not worn it yesterday and she wondered if he had bought it for the occasion. It was toast-colored with a red and white band around it and it was slightly too large for him.*

What saved Janis Joplin from being merely the loneliest madwoman on earth was that she could sing. What saves Flannery O'Connor from being the holiest mother on earth is that she can write.

Padgett Powell

Ten

A Scholar Tries to Get to Milledgeville

Flannery O'Connor taught us: the presence of mystery
And grace working through nature, which it utterly transcends.
So the natural way from Atlanta, I-20, is without neither grace

Nor blessing: the hope that on Georgia Highway 441,
Where I turn off, I will see good country scenes and people
As O'Connor saw them, with a superior eye.

But we live in a world where the blight of the mechanical
Offers many ways to fall. Or miss the exit,
(Exit also to Eatonton, home of Joel Chandler Harris,

Brer Rabbit, and the only air-conditioned slave cabins
In the South). My temptation is silver, streamlined,
An eighteen-wheeled behemoth

Bruising downhill at speeds upwards of eighty,
Then uphill cutting in at forty-five.
Constancy one of my virtues, I travel exactly five miles

Over the limit, cursing the mechanical
Monster breathing down my back and fishtailing
Into my path, flashing silver and slowing to taunt me

To pass. Of course I pass, spitting fire back,
Slicing at tires with my eyes. I insist on moderation,
For moderation shall be its own reward. And suppose strategy

Downhill: I will prevent speed; I will stay in the lane
With the truck. But when its grill fills my rear view
Like the wrath of God, I slip right, cowering in eddies

Of exhaust. So we have a contest of wills. I will
Not be intimidated by this truck. I will stay in its lane
Till it knows I am best. Like two species of frog—

A colorful arrow poison and an overweight bull—
We will leap down this road till one of us splatters.
The brute unnerves me, but I always fight back.

My version of the crash: I am passing a lake, and
There is no lake before the turnoff to Milledgeville. I ooze
To the shoulder and the map, my car leaking knowledge

Like oil and wounded pride. This time I have gone too far;
It's a diagonal sideroad back. For the last time the diesel
Roars by, having brought me to myself. Moonfaced, I enter

O'Connor's countryside, density of woods and red earth
Gouged and scarred, locus of junk and pride
I have to wander, knowing I've gone wrong.

Susan Elizabeth Howe

Flannery
O'Connor's
father,
Edward Francis
O'Connor.

Flannery O'Connor,
age three, with her
mother, Regina Cline
O'Connor, in Savannah,
Georgia, 1928.

O'Connor, age three, in Savannah, 1928. She was a creative child and loved to draw.

O'Connor, age twelve, in 1937, the year her father was diagnosed with disseminated lupus erythematosus and the year the O'Connors moved to Milledgeville, Georgia, her mother's ancestral home.

O'Connor (far left) at a neighbor's birthday party in Milledgeville, circa 1938. The O'Connors then lived in the Cline House, a large antebellum residence a few blocks from Georgia State College for Women (GSCW).

O'Connor, circa 1942, the year she graduated from Peabody High School in Milledgeville and the year she entered GSCW.

O'Connor, circa 1944, during her college days at GSCW, where she earned a B.A. in Social Science in 1945.

O'Connor (right) holding *The Corinthian*, the quarterly literary magazine of GSCW, 1944. One of O'Connor's cartoons appears on the cover.

O'Connor (seated, center) with the staff of *The Corinthian* during her tenure as editor, 1944–1945.

O'Connor, circa 1945. She attended the Iowa Writers' Workshop from 1945–1947 and earned an M.F.A. from the State University of Iowa.

O'Connor at the autograph party for *Wise Blood* given by the GSCW library staff at the Ina Dillard Russell Library in 1952.

The farmhouse at Andalusia, the family farm on the outskirts of Milledgeville.
O'Connor and her mother moved here after she was diagnosed with disseminated
lupus erythematosus in 1951.

O'Connor, circa 1957,
the year she received
a grant from the
National Institute of
Arts and Letters.

A public relations photo of O'Connor used by Georgia State College for Women in the late 1950s.

One of O'Connor's beloved peacocks on the back porch roof at Andalusia.

Eleven

O'Connor And Current Fiction

Asked if Flannery O'Connor's work has been an influence on my own fiction, I would answer yes, though not in a way that could be called direct. I had published one novel before I first encountered her on the written page and this encounter did little to excite me. I simply did not get it. As Allen Tate put it in his earliest appraisal of her work, she was "too flat-footed." Later, as did Tate, I seriously revised my opinion and became a fan. What I had begun to see was that her metaphysical stance, sharing in and magnifying the fundamental vision of the previous generation of Southern writers, was the source of a strength rapidly diminishing in the work of her immediate contemporaries. This is to say that in contrast to the latter as a whole, she viewed human experience from a strictly moral and spiritual perspective.

What was happening (and rapidly continues to happen) was an increasingly pervasive tendency to reject this vision to which O'Connor adhered and to embrace the view that human experience is wholly contained within material limits. The consequences, for fiction as for life generally, require, in order to be made persuasively clear, extensive treatment not possible in the space allowed here. But I will risk a fragmentary summary of my argument.

First is the seemingly relentless movement toward the destruction of traditional morality. It is a movement that appears bent on normalizing, indeed 'moralizing' immorality. In defense of this statement I would cite as most persuasive a particular instance relating to our current use of the language. A very short list out of many possible words will illustrate. *Shame, authority, respectability; disgrace, guilt, manliness; inhibition, repression, punishment; ostracism, sin, religion*: these are some of the names of things that now among so many people are held to be bad, unhealthy and otherwise, and advocates of this opinion would like to arrange it so that the world will be cleansed of the things and of their names as well. Repression is bad because it stifles self-expression. Respectability is a term of contempt. Authority . . . who has it? Guilt is bad for mental health. And religion? As an outworn creed of mythic origin, it belongs in the dustbin of history. Today the words of St. Paul have among our intellectual elite about the same moral authority as those of our typical televangelists.

This development, though working toward the reconstruction of our minds and indeed our human nature, would surely not, even in its ultimate fulfillment, leave a total moral vacuum. But the ideals, or values, currently recommended—equality, freedom, brotherhood, for instance—are of the most abstract kind and more than probably would leave a landscape denuded of fundamental moral goods. And I think it is already plain to most thoughtful people that lack of discipline, incivility, disarray in the family, cynicism and other evils have penetrated deep in our society, so that it is at least an open question whether they can now be eradicated.

But the afflictions of a society are the afflictions of its writers too, and it is writers (of fiction, in this case) that I am concerned with here. Among these, all too many have in some measure absorbed a condition of spirit that is most accurately described as nihilistic. This condition inevitably has consequences in their practice, and one of these consequences is the fact that the writers' choices of subject are seriously diminished. Novels in the mold of those by Henry James, Joseph Conrad, and William Faulkner, depending as they do on assumed concrete values, must surely lose all standing. Not that these three writers subscribed equally to traditional moral assumptions. But in general they took them seriously and did not hesitate to build whole novels upon or around them, novels into whose texts these values, and their contraries, were consciously or unconsciously woven. Imagine James, whose novels are novels of manners, stripped of his assumption that envy and pride and deceit are serious evils. Or consider Conrad's *Lord Jim*. A more modern Jim would likely examine his guilt in light of today's psychology textbooks and dismiss it as unjustified. And what about adultery? Today, or anyway by tomorrow, Hawthorne's Hester Prynne would, after not much reflection, rip off that scarlet "A" mainly on grounds that it disfigured her attire.

Further, without the living presence of these fundamental assumptions, the means of developing fictional character are significantly limited. In more instances than not, a character is made vividly real for us by his words and actions. Usually these must be judged as good or bad, either in themselves or for the character as a person. But if the virtue or virtues in question are not thought of as such, what do we learn about the character?

Finally, and centrally, there is the matter of the writer's vision. I am maintaining that his true vision is of a kind that passes beyond mere observation, that is able to see the world of our daily experience in the light of potential meaning. This is achieved through an act of faith by the writer, and such a writer's immediate subject, that part of the material world he has chosen to deal with in the process of reflecting his vision, assumes what may be said to resemble the power of speech. But what has the world to say to the writer who confronts it with nothing but his questions? Its answer will be silence, or at best a murmur. True vision calls the material world into the human order and gives it eloquence. Through such vision it is invested with a life that, if not wholly comprehensible, is at least mysterious.

In evidence for this and other of my points I return to Flannery O'Connor, who spent the greater part of her thirty-nine years on a farm in central Georgia. In place of an intellectual environment, she had about her, ready and natural to her hand, images of fire, water, earth and air, and, above all, the powerful vision inspired by her Roman Catholic faith. It is made manifest in ways both small and great; in the darkly threatening image of a tree-line beyond an open pasture, a brooding mystic silence over water still as glass. But we experience it most fully, of course, in the over-all thrust of her stories and novels. In my view, the famous story "A Good Man Is Hard to Find" is one of the best examples.

A Georgia family, including the grandmother, sets out on a vacation. By the grandmother's typical manipulation they make a wrong turn and on a lonely country road have an accident that overturns their car. Shortly afterwards they find themselves in the presence of an escaped convict, a pathological killer who calls himself The Misfit because, in his words, "I can't make what all I done wrong fit what all I gone through in punishment." He proceeds, with the aid of his two henchmen, to murder the family one by one, including finally, after a long and terrifying conversation, the grandmother.

The family are an unlovely lot, unsettlingly familiar. Without manners or mutual respect, without any real uniting bond, they are manipulated by the deceitful grandmother, who is forever mouthing pietisms and praising the past when good men were easy to find. They are a family as unleavened by any presence of the spiritual as a TV sit-com.

O'Connor's description of The Misfit is generally that of the sinister red-neck of folklore, but with one important exception: he wears a pair of silver-rimmed glasses that give him a scholarly look. This is a clue. A scholar is one who seeks to know the nature of reality, and this is what The Misfit has tried to do. By the time we reach the end of his conversation with the grandmother, we are prepared to see not only why he is the way he is but also why he—with such sudden violence—murders her. He has been everywhere, scrupulously observing, always seeking in vain to find some meaning in it all. But his rigorous gaze has shown him only a world that is like the penitentiary where he was held for a crime he cannot remember, a prison house in which we suffer confinement without reason. To this vision of life The Misfit, with his powerful but frustrated instinct for reason and justice, has responded like Milton's Satan: "Save what is in destroying,/ Other joy to me is lost." In The Misfit's words: "No pleasure but meanness."

The Misfit's immediate cause for killing the grandmother is a gesture she makes toward him. Moments before, dazed with terror, she mumbles some words about Jesus and his rising from the dead. They are words that make The Misfit cry out in anger and frustration against the injustice that he had not been there to see it with his own eyes. "If I had of been there I would of known and I wouldn't be like I am now." To which the grandmother replies, on sudden inspiration, "Why you're one of my babies. You're one of my own children!" It is then that he suddenly and brutally murders her.

The reason for The Misfit's violent response is this:

Given his image of himself, her words and her touching, blessing him, amount to an intolerable insult, for hereby she includes him with herself among the world's family of vulgarians, the multitude who can live their lives without ever once asking why. This, his search for truth, his honesty, are the source of his pride. One of her kind, indeed! He is the "good man" whose absence she has lamented.

In essence the story is a devastating sermon against the faithlessness of modern generations, man bereft of the spirit. This condition, portrayed in the grossness and vacuity of the vacationing family, unrelieved by the pious and sentimental prattle of the grandmother, brings their end upon them. The Misfit enters, not by coincidence but by a logic implicit in lives made grotesque when vision has departed. He, O'Connor tells us, is the fierce avenger our souls beget upon our innocent nihilism.

As I see it, O'Connor is one of only a tiny few Southern writers who survived—with strong faith intact—the rapid diminishment after World War II of the older vision that had informed the work of the Fugitive/Agrarian generation. Not that those writers were uniformly orthodox believers. But, as Lewis P. Simpson has astutely observed, shared among them generally was a fundamental assumption that individual human beings are participants in the mystery of a universal drama of good and evil directed by some kind of divinity beyond man's understanding. John Crowe Ransom, a key figure in that flowering of Southern letters in the 1920s and 1930s, regardless of his attitude toward Christian orthodoxy, wrote convincingly on the subject in his book *God Without Thunder*. He spoke of the necessity of referring man's existence to the power of a mysterious and omnipotent god, urging that such an assumption is necessary for the sake of social and psychic order, and also for the existence of poetry and art. It was in light of such a perspective that these writers undertook to explore the meaning of the South as a microcosmic image of the history of the western world. And it was this that gave to the writings of those men and women the memorable resonance they still have for us.

This resonance, I am afraid, has largely disappeared from our writing, Southern and otherwise. Through the 1950s and 1960s there were talented writers who, feeling a continuity with the older sensibility, endeavored to follow in their predecessors' footsteps. But for most it was only to find that those old assumptions had loosened their hold on the imagination. This realization signaled the essentially new departures that characterize Southern writing today, departures that have brought it more nearly in line with the outlook in regions far other than the South. This is not meant to suggest that Southern writing has lost all its old virtues. Still surviving in considerable degree among the best of Southern writers is an interest in the local, in history, and also in myth, a form that transcendence can take. Nor is there any lack of genuine talent. As to fiction, in my probably biased opinion, present-day Southern writers need not defer to, and likely have an edge over writers of any other region of the country. Even so, present-day readers must listen in vain for the sound of that old departed thunder, so clearly audible in O'Connor's fiction.

Madison Jones

Twelve

Retrospective

for Flannery's friend, Louise Abbot

When you come to remember
As of course you must
The sun will wear the look of yesterday
Crayoned, lowering, below the edge of blue
That is sky, above the line of trees
Which were only words she used,
A way of moving towards
The stillness at the center
Beyond the pond, the eternal
Anticipation and your car
Crackling its tires on the dry road
Leading from your house to hers
Which was not her house at all
(Place is always somewhere else)
But one she could draw well:

The sloping porch, its opaque screens,
Herself at the top of the steps
Above yard hens and bright birds
Whose plumage changed the seasons
Whose cry evoked your leaving
Before the clock struck five
The hour she need not color
That word she need not speak
Against the dimming of the landscape
When she would be, in your remembering,
Most nearly herself

Sarah Gordon

Thirteen

An Enduring Chill

"A Good Man Is Hard to Find," "Everything That Rises Must Converge," "Parker's Back," "Judgment Day"—many of O'Connor's stories resonate years after my first reading of them. I've asked myself why. I've contemplated what brings me back to them. I've wondered what, as a poet, I've learned from their lessons—the lessons O'Connor hid in them in the way all great writers unknowingly hide instructions for aspiring ones.

Relatively speaking, a poet has little room to work in. This is one of the comparisons often made with prose writers—less space, fewer words. But is the job of the prose writer really so different? All writers depend on *le mot juste,* the precisely accurate detail, the telling moment described in language at once commonplace and profound. If the poet has less room in which to stretch, the burdens are that much greater, the pressure on compelling language that much more deciding.

What do we remember of our own lives? Not the generalized truths we've garnered from lived experience, but the particulars of that experience, those often rather ordinary sensory essentials that render an experience indelibly memorable. Your high school boyfriend breaks up with you. Years later you remember not his words, but the single thread protruding from the pair of torn jeans you wore that day, the way the thread felt as you wound it round and round an index finger.

When I consider O'Connor's fiction, I realize that what has stayed with me are her curiously ordinary details, those dimples imbedded in the surfaces of her stories that anchor them in the world I recognize as my own, that render them irresistibly unforgettable. I still see Asbury Fox's naive mother in the opening of "The Enduring Chill" as she is startled by her morbidly dramatic son's bloodshot left eye, and later the apparently ailing young man's vision of Dr. Block's "asinine face . . . as senseless as a baby's." I remember Lucynell's and her mother's violent rocking on the porch on either side of Mr. Shiftlet in "The Life You Save May Be Your Own." Nor can I forget the "red-rimmed and pale and defenseless-looking" eyes of The Misfit without his glasses at the close of "A Good Man Is Hard to Find"—the eyes of the same man whose "silver-rimmed spectacles . . . gave him a scholarly look" at his first entrance into the story. I remember the way the sky behaves in so many of O'Connor's stories, the way the natural world seems always to echo the minutiae of the human lives that carry on within it.

In such details O'Connor's narratives resound. And it is specifically because of these details—singly standing for much more than themselves but without which the stories would dissolve—that the narratives endure. And so it has to be with poems, I realized: detail, image—created as though from the inside out. And this is another of O'Connor's lessons: One cannot impose such elements. What is *true* must rise (and converge) from one's honest portrayal of characters and of the world in which the writer discovers them. The writer's job, be she poet or fiction writer, is to know this world, to inhabit even its crevasses.

What astonishes me is O'Connor's imagination, her ability to envision, to locate her stories, detail by detail, and to deliver her characters *through* those details, emblazoning them on the psyches of her readers. O'Connor implies that she learned such tricks from reading Flaubert. In "The Nature and Aim of Fiction" she quotes a sentence from his *Madame Bovary* in which Emma's piano playing is heard by a bailiff's clerk on the other side of the village. O'Connor remarks on the importance that Flaubert gives to incorporating the detail that the clerk is wearing his "list slippers," and she suggests that all writers be as concerned as the French novelist with creating such "a believable village to put Emma in."

In this essay O'Connor goes on to distinguish between literalism and naturalism. She insists that art must be selective, not inclusive (as life is) so as to *seem* like life in its essence and truth. The detail that is essential, she says, is the one that "creates movement." How does a poet choose such essential detail? How does she recognize it? After thirty years of creating poems, I am still learning.

And so I continue to read O'Connor—her lectures and essays and letters, but mainly her fiction, in part for the pleasures of her prose and in part because she continues to be an important mentor. Only rarely does literature resound as though it were lived life. O'Connor's fiction, in fact, reminds me to pay attention to my writing, knowing that if I will succeed in my writing I must not only listen to the world but also absorb it. I must inhabit its underside. Finally, I must understand that for my work to matter, for it to be both charismatic and necessary, its language must be alert, its images fresh and honest, and its concise particulars, which may seem almost accidentally included, must deliver—with a chill of recognition—the enduring world.

Andrea Hollander Budy

Fourteen

Unholy Sonnet

for Flannery O'Connor

He loads his weapons, but the Lord God sees him.
He hears the inner voice that tells him, "Yes,"
The voice that tells him, "No." And the Lord sees him,
Watching as he listens first to one voice,
A melody, then the other, like a latch
That slips and catches, slips, until it clicks.
The Lord God sees the hard decision taken,
Watching with His seven compound eyes,
As intimate as starlight, as detached.
He sees between the victims and the killer
Each angle of trajectory. Unshaken,
He sees the horror dreamed and brought to being
And still maintains His vigil and His power,
Which you and I would squander with a scream.

Mark Jarman

Fifteen

Flannery & Other Regions

I t's frustrating to write about Flannery in an anonymous voice: because she was such a master at digging from the particular to reach the universal, it's disconcerting to have to approach her from the opposite direction, to have to respond to a specific life and work in global terms. Fiction is a considered gift from one sensibility that shapes to another that actively receives. So who speaks here?

To say that I am a black woman artist using the name of Alma Thomas—a dead black woman artist—so as to "fight sexism and racism in the art world" (the official line of the Guerrilla Girls) is to tell you almost nothing, either about the me who makes art or the me who reads Flannery. It reduces me to the very thing I oppose, a stereotype.

Flannery understood that no one is a cipher, the mere "representative" of a category. She more than most would have realized how limiting it is not to reveal the date and place of my birth, not to describe the accent in which my parents spoke (different from mine) and the style of their manners (more refined), not to hint at the peculiar psychic history they passed on to me (if only they hadn't); or, to peel the onion further, not to be able to tell you whom I married, how I've earned a living, my education. . . . I'm convinced Flannery would have sympathized and would read these global statements remembering their missing nuance, and that gives me the courage to proceed. However, I'll have to restrict myself to her nonfiction; responding with less than my whole self to her fiction, even if it were possible, would be too disheartening.

The thirty-five years since Flannery died have been so critical for the culture, a period in which the magnitude of change in society has seemed even greater than that in individuals. It's hard to avoid "presentist" projection with respect to her. Five years before she died, I had my first encounter with Flannery, in a yellow cloth book with *Wise Blood* in big letters on the cover that a friend had bought me from a remainder bin—a first edition I no longer have and wish I did. Looking back, I think that in most ways I haven't changed much since then, and perhaps in the basics not at all. Yet the culture has changed so greatly that backwardly interrogating Flannery about this or that new perspective is like asking one of those historical impersonators, "What would Mr. Jefferson think?" There is always the danger of either giving her the benefit of every doubt, based on the love one had at first sight, or dismissing her as irrelevant.

For years after my first encounter, I read Flannery "bi-optically," interpolating my reality into hers. How could it have been otherwise when I did not feel part of the audience she anticipated? Peeking through a keyhole, "overhearing" the work, seeing but not being seen, turned the work into a secret all the more delicious. But two decades later, having consumed most of her fiction, I confess that picking up her essays and lectures came as a relief. Here was an explicit statement of authorial intentions that provided me a firm handle; instead of evanescent images, there were concrete ideas with which I could agree or disagree, and best of all, there was an explanation of the love I continued to feel.

For me, *Mystery and Manners* came at a crucial moment; I found it shortly after I'd come out as a visual artist. I felt I was standing inside a room we shared—not engaging with Flannery as an equal, of course, but getting there. Still, two decades had passed since my first reading of her fiction, and now the room looked different; it had been rearranged by shifts in the culture—not the least of which had been the revolutionary black women's writing that had created a new audience for literature. I wondered: would Flannery's work and ideas survive the changes I could now see? The answer was an unequivocal yes, but with massive ironies I hoped she was enjoying.

To get the negative out of the way first, in a 1959 letter to Maryat Lee, Flannery wrote something that at this distance feels frankly embarrassing. Responding to a proposed meeting with James Baldwin, she said: "No I can't see James Baldwin in Georgia. It would cause the greatest trouble and disturbance and disunion. In New York it would be nice to meet him; here it would not. I observe the traditions of the society I feed on—it's only fair. Might as well expect a mule to fly as me to see James Baldwin in Georgia."

When you imagine the plane of intellectual camaraderie on which the out gay and black Baldwin wanted to meet the virginal Flannery, it's hard not to be sad that she couldn't rise to his level. She was sick, of course, and conserving her

75

energy, not just choosing her battles but no doubt trying to avoid them. Still, it makes me cringe.

For all Flannery's interest in the eternal, the transcendent, the universal, she understood the need for distinctions; and she tried to see through them, not overcome them. She said to an interviewer: "I have a talk I sometimes give called 'The Catholic Novelist in the Protestant South' and I find that the title makes a lot of people. . .nervous. Why bring up the distinction? Particularly when the word Christian ought to settle both." Most hyphenated Americans have heard a version of this objection. "The distinctions between the Catholic and Protestant are distinctions within the same family," she went on, "but every distinction is important to the novelist. Distinctions of belief create distinctions of habit, distinctions of habit make for distinctions of feeling. You don't believe on one side of your head and feel on the other."

It's true that times would change. "Distinctions" would become "differences." But between distinctions of belief and differences in experience there is a short distance, one it's clear that Flannery was large enough to encompass.

She once said, "The best American writing has always been regional." But since she wrote this, the concept of "region" has itself been redefined; it now includes not only geographic but cultural borders. It's hard for some of us to lament television's flattening of the old Southern and Midwestern literatures when so many new regions of black, gay, and immigrant writing have since vibrantly entered the space. I believe the writer who made even black readers love "The Artificial Nigger" could have become reconciled to this change.

There's no need to rewrite the past. Flannery could never have predicted that those who soon would need her more than air would be the very readers and writers who'd been so marginalized she couldn't imagine them as part of her audience. It is her embattlement as a believing writer in a secular world and the morality of her aesthetic standards that have instructed generations of artists who have been "othered." Whenever I reread *Mystery and Manners*, I picture dozens of artists underlining, writing in the margins, changing the word Catholic to Asian, lesbian, Latino. This is an irony I feel Flannery would relish in time.

In addition, political similarities have resonated in aesthetic solutions. From the Southern grotesque that Flannery's work embodied and described to the postcolonial magic realism of García Márquez and Rushdie seems a hop, skip, and a jump. She wrote: "When you can assume that your audience holds the same beliefs you do, you can relax a little and use more normal means of talking to it; when you have to assume that it does not, then you have to make your vision apparent by shock—to the hard of hearing you shout, and for the almost-blind you draw large and startling figures." This could be sisterly advice to Toni Morrison.

I grant that many aspects of Flannery's thought (perhaps even her fiction, though I think not) may appear superficially dated. Though I believe she deserves infinite reading generosity, others may find their patience tried. What remains that is irreducible? As a nation, we have become aware that competing narratives broaden and deepen our understanding, that inflecting the story of Thomas Jefferson with that of Sally Hemings (and vice versa) helps us see both more clearly. I believe that Flannery's art and thought have been strengthened by—but can never be replaced by—Morrison's.

Although Flannery valued regional writing, she also noted that "to be regional in the best sense you have to see beyond the region." She did not intend this *beyond* to mean *outside*: neither Sophocles, Murasaki, Chaucer, nor Tolstoy saw *outside* their region, or had to.

"The Southern writer is forced from all sides to make his gaze extend beyond the surface, beyond mere problems, until it touches that realm which is the concern of prophets and poets," she wrote in *Mystery and Manners*. The *beyond* that is a *beneath*, the openness to the unexpected and availability to mystery that she practiced in her art and preached in her essays, stands, I believe, as her warning beacon to the regional artists who continue to come after her. It's one we will always be guided and daunted by.

Guerrilla Girl Alma Thomas

Sixteen

Flannery O'Connor, Old Testament Christian Storyteller

I have had a long, troubled, but ultimately rewarding relationship with the
fiction of Flannery O'Connor. As a humanist, I have always
been repelled by what I feel to be Flannery O'Connor's mean-
spiritedness. As both an agnostic and now as a recently converted Protestant Christian, I am offended by my sense of her
version of Catholic superiority. As a writer and a teacher, I
have always been struck by what I've considered the crudeness
of her use of the techniques of fiction, especially the omniscient point of view. Having read her novels and most of her
stories (several times over), I am compelled, finally, to testify to
the uniqueness of her vision and her raw storytelling power.

I have been struggling with my attitude toward her as a
person and a writer ever since I became actively aware of her
in 1960 while teaching stories in *The House of Fiction,* edited
by Allen Tate and Caroline Gordon. I disdainfully declined
to teach "A Good Man Is Hard to Find." But later, a col-

league who was co-editing a textbook with me included this O'Connor story, and I let his choice remain. Later, having taught it often, I ended up regarding it as one of the great short stories. In another text I included "Good Country People," and in yet another, I included both versions of "Geranium," later rewritten and published as the story "Judgment Day." Her ironic vision enabled O'Connor—from the beginning, as in "Geranium"—to delineate the absurdities of racial prejudice.

I respect her for having revised a good number of stories after first publication. An examination of "Geranium," a later revision, "An Exile in the East," and the final version, "Judgment Day," in which the original story is radically reconceived and seven pages longer than the first versions, reveals not only that she greatly matured as an artist, but also that her vision of black-white relationships in the South and the North had become more complex. Information in the Library of America edition of her collected works facilitates such a fascinating comparison. I like to imagine the pleasure it must have been for her to employ her mature talent to revise and improve this story after twenty years—and great fame. Her effort is a dramatic demonstration of a writer's compulsion to "get it right." But this revision story is an exceptional case. I know of no other writer who has rewritten a first published story after so many years, and certainly no one who, in failing health, knew that this version would likely be her final published story.

I am surprised to realize today that so many of the O'Connor stories which aggravate the fool out of me, even enrage me, sometimes make me sad to know that such a sensibility as hers was loose in the world, finally command and hold my attention and compel rereading: for example,

"The Train," "The Life You Save May Be Your Own," "The River," "The Displaced Person," "The Artificial Nigger," "Greenleaf," "Revelation," "Parker's Back," and "Everything That Rises Must Converge." That I am repelled, irritated, enraged, and saddened by what seems to be her holier-than-thou arrogance, while I yet spend a fair amount of my life on earth living in the world she has created, probably makes me kin to the legion of perverse and grotesque characters she has created. Someday, I'll try to understand that, but here I want to be specific about the work itself, looking at stories I perversely cherish.

I am keenly aware that O'Connor never allowed any of her characters to tell their own stories in the first person. I speculate that it was a matter of temperament that compelled her to cleave profoundly to the all-knowing (omniscient) point of view. She was already tending toward omniscience in the first story in her thesis collection, "The Geranium." The point of view is basically third person, central intelligence (I prefer this term coined by Henry James over "limited"), but she veers away from it now and then, as she continued to do in "Judgment Day." In two of her most powerful stories, "Good Country People" and "A Good Man Is Hard to Find," she arbitrarily shifts focus from one character to another within the omniscient point of view.

Of course, O'Connor's weapons of irony and paradox *can* be employed in first person and in central intelligence, but my reading of her works gives me the impression that her power to overwhelm us is generated by the intensity of her focus on her vision, a Jeremiah-like Old Testament revision of the Gospels of the New Testament. Reading her fiction sometimes makes me doubt that she ever really heard the Good News. She's like the fundamentalist evangelist on campus who points at students passing, shouting, "Whores like you are going straight to hell," except that she favors as satirical targets such grotesque people as that evangelist. As she ridicules fire-and-brimstone Protestant Christians, I feel scorched by and smell brimstone coming from her own sensibility.

Turn to the first paragraph of "The Displaced Person," and you will hear O'Connor strike a note of contempt and ridicule: "The peacock was following Mrs. Shortley up the road to the hill where she meant to stand." That's the set-up, here's the put-down: "She stood on two tremendous legs, with the grand self-confidence of a mountain, and rose, up narrowing bulges of granite, to two icy blue points of light that pierced forward, surveying everything."

Even as she begins to create her character—before I know anything on which to judge her—the all-knowing author insists that I sneer at Mrs. Shortley even as Mrs. Shortley herself, a few passages later, sneers at other characters: "watching from her vantage point" she "had the sudden intuition that the Gobblehooks, like rats with typhoid fleas, could have carried all those murderous ways over the water with them to this place." Note the names the creator gives her creatures. The words O'Connor chooses to describe Mrs. Shortley are no less meanspirited than Mrs. Shortley's chosen words for the Gobblehooks. For O'Connor, it's as though, "in the beginning was the Word and the Word tears the flesh." Given my perception of the fact that O'Connor is one of the most overtly judgmental of writers in all literature, I have to feel that she is appealing to the lowest impulses in me.

And I prefer not to. But I read her anyway—the writer I love to hate and hate to love. Until I became a Christian. How that has affected my own judgment of her I will understand by and by.

In the first twenty pages of this shape-shifting story, I find twenty examples of O'Connor's negative feelings about her own creations. That's typical of my experience reading most of her stories. With O'Connor, we judge Mrs. Shortley— and soon with Mrs. Shortley, we judge the "Gobblehooks." This ambiguity is, of course, one source of her power: just as I judge this, that, and the other way, I am sinking in my own moral, psychological, spiritual quicksand, and if I am astute enough I realize that. The old Milton routine all over again: Satan is more attractive than Christ and that's how Paradise got lost, over and over again in each human heart. By the end of this story, O'Connor's strident omniscience provokes in me a response that can only be called "transcendent." A note I made at the end of that story only suggests what even now I cannot articulate fully: "Flannery O'Connor resembles the dispassionate Angel of Death."

"A Good Man Is Hard to Find" is, in my view, O'Connor's ✳ greatest parable. The omniscient narrator points satirically at the superficially religious grandmother whose mechanical religiosity gets her shot when she encounters the escaped convict. O'Connor seems to make the point that a killer whose beliefs are shaped clearly in suffering is in some ways spiritually superior to a comical old lady like the grandmother. Like Manley Pointer in "Good Country People," The Misfit is not ridiculed by his creator. My response to that is this: to deal with the dilemma of depicting a character whose spiritual life is at ground zero, as the grandmother's is, presents a challenge to all of us fiction writers that is so great we shrink back from it without hesitation. True, Christ himself was more drawn to sinners like the killer than to sinners like the old woman, but I don't even want to think—not right now anyway—about the implications of that. O'Connor expended her satirical wrath on human targets of small consequence, on the one hand, and so in great need of compassion, on the other.

Of course, O'Connor is never as simple as I have suggested. In one of my textbooks, following "A Good Man Is Hard to Find," I posed these two ironic paradoxes: "The result of the grandmother's and The Misfit's actions; the killer saves one of his victims, the grandmother, by shooting her; the grandmother tries to save herself, but may have helped to save the killer's soul." In O'Connor's parables, killers and con men are paradoxically savior figures. But in this story, The Misfit needs the grandmother, it appears, for his own salvation.

And sometimes, as a person and as a person who is a writer, I think I need O'Connor like I need a hole in the head; but sometimes I think that is exactly what I need, and O'Connor is only too happy to oblige me.

When, years ago, I heard that O'Connor lived with her mother, kept peacocks on her farm, and was slowly dying of lupus down in the red hills of Georgia, the very image of her, melancholy but romantic somehow, appealed to me and made her a vivid presence in my imagination. Driving north from Florida one dark and stormy night, I pulled off the highway and slept in the Milledgeville Holiday Inn. O'Connor had died, but I wanted to lay my eyes on that farm with its peacocks. "Can you tell me how to get to Flannery O'Connor's farm?" The young waiter said he never heard of her. An elderly lady overheard, pulled at my coattail, and I followed the directional gesture she made to a farm directly across the highway, where a rutted driveway climbed a forlorn-faced slope, the morning sun gleaming on a roof like a brow.

Something else made me feel close to O'Connor. My friend Peggy Bach had lupus and was trying, in pain, to finish a biography of Evelyn Scott, so we often talked of O'Connor, suffering and writing.

"What's the matter?" I sometimes asked Peggy.

"The wolf is on the prowl in my bloodstream."

Now that I think of them both in the same sentence, they were a lot alike, those two. Once Peggy told me, "You are a fool." She said this with a straight face a month before she died of liver cancer. I learned the hard way that she and O'Connor did not suffer fools gladly.

David Madden

Seventeen

On Reading & Rereading Flannery O'Connor

I remember—the way I remember the day President Kennedy was shot—the first time I read a story by Flannery O'Connor. It was in 1953 when Southern white women had cooks. Together, my cook Hattie and I had cooked and served a typical noonday farm meal of meat, fresh vegetables, hot bread, and homemade dessert. A morning's work.

I took Hattie home and came back for an hour of rest. With me was the new issue of *Harper's Bazaar,* which published fiction at the time. The story I read was "A Late Encounter With The Enemy."

I was electrified. When I saw the word "guls" for "girls," I felt a stab of pure envy. No writer had penned down Southern speech in that way. The characters were so real, familiar, funny, and tragic that I felt present at Sally Poker Sash's graduation, saw the General on the stage in his wheelchair, the irresponsible Boy Scout behind him. At the end, the General was disposed of with two words, *the corpse.* Brilliant, I thought.

Because I'm neither critic nor scholar, I didn't take the story apart or go into its meaning. I simply loved it. And I felt that Flannery O'Connor had split contemporary American fiction into some kind of Before and After.

I had only one doubt that day. Could she do it again? I watched for her work everywhere, followed her career with consuming interest. When she died, I knew that her work would not die with her.

I thought I knew the stories fairly well, but when I read "Late Encounter" again, then some of the less anthologized stories that I only half-remembered, I found that I knew little more than the surface of her work. This time I got, in a personal way, the hard underlying religious message, and it's scary. She gave us fictional prophets because she was a prophet.

In stories like "The Comforts of Home" and "The Partridge Festival," her message seems a little forced to me now, though it feels almost blasphemous to say so. She pushes to incredible extremes, but her genius sweeps the reader along unblinking—as people have fits in a doctor's office, get beaten on the back over a fresh tattoo, have mystical experiences while hosing down a pig parlor.

How could I have let her books sit on my shelves—even beside Faulkner, Joyce, Flaubert, where I keep them—all this time? I'm reading her again, trying to learn to write fiction and to save my soul.

Mary Ward Brown

Eighteen

There Is No Such Thing as "The Writer"

The assignment here—one I readily accepted, one I am honored beyond measure to have accepted—is to find a few words on Flannery O'Connor in an appreciation of her work. Anything I want to write, I have been told by the editor, and now that I am here, the truth is I can tell you anything I want.

I could write, for instance, about Boy Scout Troop 20, over at Mt. Pleasant Presbyterian—I am an assistant scoutmaster—and how when we went backpacking in the Pisgah National Forest a year and a half ago, I was afraid both my sons—Zeb, then age fourteen, and Jacob, twelve—though avid campers, might find it awfully difficult to hike the seven miles up to the top of Shining Rock. They hadn't actually backpacked before, and the trail climbed 3500 feet in elevation over those seven miles, ending at the mountaintop and 6000 feet. Of course, as their father, I was afraid they'd get whipped, tired out, start whining, and even I gave them a stern lecture before we headed up the trail about the need for patience, for stamina, for not being whiners when the trail got tough.

I could write of how I was stunned, however, when, nearing the top of the mountain, me dead last, bringing up the rear and feeling that I was about to die, I looked up the trail and saw Zeb taking the backpack off one of the younger kids who had all but given up, the boy sobbing on the trailside because of how heavy his pack was and how tired he was and how we would never get to the campsite. I watched my son put that younger boy's backpack over his own shoulder, then look back down the trail at me, and ask, "Dad, you all right?"

I nodded, out of breath, unable to say a word, and watched him turn, head on up the mountain, two backpacks on now, one on each shoulder. He'd already pitched his tent by the time I made it to camp.

And during these few pages handed over to me in good faith I would talk about O'Connor. I could tell you about my other son, Jacob, who stunned me on this same campout as well, the two of us sharing a tent at the top of this mountain on a night that got down to eleven degrees. I'd spent myself that day, so exhausted by the time I climbed into the tent with Jake that I didn't even want to refill my canteen from the spring someone'd found up there. I'd drunk all my water on the way up, and when in the middle of the night I wanted more water and knew I had none, I asked Jake if he had any.

He said he did and got out his canteen. In the bottom of it was only a dribble, enough to wet a parched mouth. But this was my son's water I was about to drain, and so I asked him if he wanted it.

"No," he said. "You take it. I can wait till morning."

And I drank it.

And I could tell you, too, of the mystery of how every time I get up in the middle of the night for a drink of water now, I think of Jacob as I stand in the darkness at the sink, the cup to my lips, and that night in a tent, the wind on a North Carolina mountaintop tracing through the trees above us while I drank the last of my son's water, and I think of Zeb, too, and his taking that kid's backpack and checking on me, and I am thankful and puzzled at once: given a father like me, one who'd underestimated his kids, who figured they'd end up whining and whipped; given *me*, how is it they turned out like that?

But if I were to tell you about all this as my way of filling my allotted space here, you might get the idea I wasn't paying attention to the occasion at hand: an appreciation of Flannery O'Connor. You might think I was a little nuts, even, if I were to go on any more about my boys, and I haven't even started in about my wife, Melanie, whom I love and still can't figure out after nineteen years of marriage, that inability to figure her out one of the great mysteries about her I love.

But there's a reason I'm not talking about what you may think I ought to be talking about. Namely, O'Connor. And it's this: I know nothing.

It's true. My having been asked to write this for such an august occasion, and now the fact of my writing it, makes me more than apprehensive because, after having written five novels, two story collections, and a memoir, I believe now more than ever what Socrates said quite a while ago: "the greatest level of wisdom man can hope to attain is the realization of how little he knows."

Not only is this notion Socratic, it is also Biblical: Proverbs 13:10 says "Through presumption comes nothing but strife, but with those who receive counsel is wisdom."

And I believe now more than ever this same notion given us by O'Connor herself, her words my path into the life of writing—a habit of art—such as the one I have been blessed enough to lead. "There's a grain of stupidity that the writer of fiction can hardly do without," she writes in "The Nature and Aim of Fiction," "and this is the quality of having to stare, of not getting the point at once."

The essay, from *Mystery and Manners,* has served as a cornerstone for my writing life. I know that sounds inflated, hyperbolic, perhaps even nauseatingly effusive. But I tell you the unabashed truth: that essay, and indeed the entire book, has been a shelter to which I repair more and more often the longer I write, and the longer I teach writing. Because the longer I do both, the more I realize how very true her words ring: "In the first place," she writes in the essay as a means to address the audience at hand, a creative writing class called "How the Writer Writes" to which she has been invited to speak, "there is no such thing as *the* writer, and I think that if you don't know that now, you should by the time such a course as this is over. In fact, I predict that it is the one thing you can be absolutely certain of learning."

This not knowing—this exacting and unforgiving and necessary grain of stupidity—has always pervaded my writing life, a mysterious gift I have wrestled with all along, precisely because the world would have us all believe that writing is a premeditated act, a kind of written death penalty of Story it is left to the hands of the writer—me—to carry out. Every novel I have written, every story or essay I have attempted, has been found only through the achingly liberating surrender of my will to the work at hand. Yet it has been O'Connor's clarion call in the crystalline prose of her essays on writing that has taught me to battle the sad and blinded belief that at times I knew what I was doing.

I was given the book *Mystery and Manners* while a grad student at the University of Massachusetts at Amherst, me nothing more than a punk kid, twenty-two and -three and -four years old, and having had visited upon me the worst curse can be given: I was told by my undergraduate teacher that I was a good writer. And, of course, I believed it.

So that my first time through the book there were only a few things I underlined, sharp daggers of truth that made me feel a little superior to the rest of my comrades in arms for the fact I saw them as piercing others I knew, and not me: "A mind cleared of false emotion and false sentiment and egocentricity is going to have at least those roadblocks removed from its path" painted precisely that bearded jerk in workshop who thought everything he wrote was gold, everything everyone else put to paper lead; "I know well enough that very few people who are supposedly interested in writing are interested in writing well" spoke plain and strong of the dimwitted woman at the end of the table who wrote nothing but bodice rippers in the guise of pallidly existentialist *New Yorker* stories; "Now in every writing class you find people who care nothing about writing, because they think they already are writers by virtue of some experience they've had" might well have been my rubber-stamped response to the bloated and boring coming-of-age novel our resident lesbian was eternally submitting for critique.

But it wasn't until I left school and started working on my own novel that I began to have the first glimmer of the deeper truths O'Connor here outlined: the notion of humility, of seeing clearly one's own motivations and desires, and the malevolently mitigating factors ego and will exert on a writer who believes there is such a thing. She was writing *of* me, it would take years to realize, and not pointing out for me truths I needed to know about others.

One Friday night in September 1984, while watching *Dallas*, I was struck with the truth that if I wanted to get a book published, I had to write a novel. I had just graduated with my MFA and a collection of stories for my thesis, and judging by the routine return of the book from every publisher I sent it to, I figured that a novel would be easier. We had moved from Northampton, Massachusetts, to Columbus, Ohio, during the summer so that I could start my first job, teaching remedial English at Ohio State University. The job was a three-year, terminal lectureship—it sounds as bad as it was—in which I taught five sections of remedial English per quarter. Sitting there watching JR nearly come to blows with Bobby while that damned oil portrait of Jock loomed on the wall of the dining room there at South Fork, I realized that in fact I'd already written the first chapter of a novel, a short story from the thesis called "This Plumber," and realized in the next moments that three other stories in the thesis could, if I fiddled enough with them, be about the same couple, snapshots out of the album of their lives

Sometimes trash TV can yield usable gifts, though I am certain O'Connor would shudder at the notion.

But the first visual past this realization of form—I needed to write a novel, and had a few components already in hand—the image that drove met to sit down and start that first novel, *The Man Who Owned Vermont*, was of an RC salesman standing in the back room of a grocery store the day after Christmas, bagboys tossing unsold Christmas trees into the huge bailing machine back there. In fact, the first extant piece of that novel is the scrawled line "Day after

Christmas—bagboys bailing Christmas trees," written on the back of an orientation letter from the remedial English department, the only piece of paper close at hand when the image came to me, JR and Bobby still tussling on the floor. That was the image I wanted in that novel, this feeling of remorse, of things already terminated and out of our hands: Christmas over, trees bailed.

It was that scene I wanted, the story to last, in my mind's eye, at least a month, from the November morning "This Plumber" takes place on through to that sad and remote ending, the day after Christmas.

The problem, though, was that I'd never written anything longer than twelve pages prior to embarking on the book. Zeb was only one year old then, and we lived in a two-bedroom townhome apartment, the two bedrooms upstairs, on the first floor a living room and a kitchen, a basement beneath it all. Each morning I got up between 4:30 and 5:00 and maneuvered my way down the stairs, careful not to step on the third step down, as that board groaned and woke up the baby every time. Then it was to the kitchen for a cup of instant coffee and a piece of toast, all by the light of the stove hood, and then down to the basement and the desk I had stationed there beneath the only window, a narrow thing six feet up that looked out onto the dirt of the flowerbed and through which I could see stars still out when I sat down at that desk.

Where sat before me an interminable amount of time to write about—a month!—when every story I'd written thus far lasted, perhaps, fifteen, twenty minutes out of a life, and involved, for the most part, a man and a woman standing in a kitchen, thinking about things.

What did I do? How could I get to that day after Christmas? How could I make time pass?

The only thing I knew to do, of course, was to start writing. This is by no means a glib answer, a jolly pitch to dismiss a genuine concern. Rather, it is the truth of what it means to be a writer: John Gardner writes in *On Becoming a Novelist*, "[I]t's the sheer act of writing, more than anything else, that makes a writer." Common sense, numskull logic. But you'd be surprised at the amount of handwringing that goes on by people who *want* to write, but are too fearful to write.

And I had a plan in my mind; I had before me those three other stories, placed them in my line of sight as though they were stepping stones across a stream. On the other side, the opposite shore, lay that final scene, the day after Christmas.

So that each writing day had a kind of goal: I wrote the next line, asking *What happens next, and what associations might that action bring to the character's mind?* with the next story my endpoint. I wanted merely to get to the next stone in the stream, that next story I'd already written, all in order to get to that far shore, the day after Christmas.

But the novel, though happily participating in this scheme, had other ideas about where it wanted to go and when, though I kept that scrawled line on my desk every day, looked at it, focused on it as a means to drive me forward through time, and though I continued to write to that next stone, the story.

Yet, during the next year it took me to write the book, the novel wrestled itself free from what I intended. Time took on its own standard, and the story and its associations only lasted from the week before Thanksgiving to the sixth of December. That opposite shore, finally, existed only in my plans, however well-meaning and heartfelt.

What I encountered, though, once I'd hit what seemed the finish of the book, was a sense that I had somehow betrayed the book, or that it had betrayed me. I wanted that last image, that Christmas tree in the bailer, and so tried to write more on to the end of the story, more lines that would lead me, despite the fact the novel had already informed me it was over, so that I could find what my will wanted to find.

And the new writing didn't work.

And here came to haunt me O'Connor's words, found back in grad school but glossed over as being the technique (or lack thereof) of a particular writer in regard to a particular story. In the essay "On Her Own Work," O'Connor writes, "I wouldn't want you to think that in that story ['Good Country People'] I sat down and said, 'Now I am going to write a story about a Ph.D. with a wooden leg, using the wooden leg as a symbol for another kind of affliction.' I doubt myself if many writers know what they are going to do when they start out. When I started writing that story, I didn't know there was going to be a Ph.D. with a wooden leg in it. I merely found myself one morning writing a description of two women that I knew something about, and before I realized it, I had equipped one of them with a daughter with a wooden leg. As the story progressed, I brought in the Bible salesman, but I had no idea what I was going to do with him. . . . This is a story that produces a shock for the reader, and I think one reason for this is that it produced a shock for the writer."

I doubt myself if many writers know what they are going to do when they start out.

Was it true? Could it be true? Could a story lead its own life, with me only some kind of conduit for it? Had my book, the one I'd planned and planned, a life of its own, out of my hands, and was that a good thing?

I abandoned the attempts to try to write to my desired end.

And the book was published with the end I arrived at all alone, in spite of my own mistrust and doubts. And, like anyone blessed with the gift of stupidity, I still hadn't learned a thing.

I started my third novel, *Jewel*, in 1989, and saw before me a story that would begin in 1943 and end, for some reason I cannot say to this day, somewhere around 1984. Again I couldn't for the life of me figure how to do it, cover time for all those years; the longest amount of time I'd covered by then was in the novel just prior to *Jewel*, *A Stranger's House*, which spanned only four months.

Yet here stood forty-one years before me, waiting to be recorded, made believable. Made *real*, when in fact if one were to engage in actually recording the fact of a life lived, attempting to make reality real, forty-one years would last more pages than I could have written in forty-one years. And still, as I looked at the beginning of my third novel—would I ever get the hang of this?—the question mocked me: how do you just get time to go by?

What would be the technique by which I would stage such an epic story? How could I pull this off? By this time I'd reread "The Nature and Aim of Fiction" so many times I'd committed to memory the line, "It's always wrong of course to say that you can't do this or you can't do that in fiction. You can do anything you can get away with, but nobody has ever gotten away with much." But what could I try to get away with?

So, armed only with the experience of having written the two novels prior to this one by simply writing them down and with my desire to tell the story of a woman who has six children, five of whom are born in a log cabin in the Mississippi wilderness, the sixth a Down Syndrome baby born in a country hospital, I started writing.

And found, around page fifty-four or so, I hadn't yet let

one day pass. I'd started before sunup this March day in 1943 and hadn't yet let go. They were only now sitting down to supper. I still had forty-one years to go, minus a day.

But, lucky for me, the light of ingenuity and inspiration also dawned on me when I realized that I could make as many years pass by as I wished, if I could only illuminate a single day out of the year I chose to skip to next. That is, this one day in 1943 could stand for her life here, now; the next section of the book, whichever year it turned out to be, would chronicle *another* single day. If I could simply tell the truth of that day, reveal what happens and the associations the details of that day bring to Jewel's mind, then I wouldn't have to worry about precisely how to get time to go by. *Time would handle itself.*

Thus I settled on a plan: this section, 1943, would be named "Monday," the next section "Tuesday," and so on, until, finally, I would reach 1984, the year with which I wanted to end Jewel's story, and call it, simply, "Sunday," the day of rest. It seemed fitting, logical, even poetic: she would be eighty years old then, her children, all six of them, including the Down Syndrome baby she had had to raise, would be grown, and she would be alone. Beautiful, I figured.

I finished the Monday section, that day ending after dark, the night going cold, in Jewel the knowledge she was going to have a sixth child. The section, finally, weighed in at around ninety manuscript pages.

I'd found my *technique.*

Then I started on "Tuesday." When I finished that section, and before, truly, I even noticed it, five months had gone by in that single section, from October and the birth of the baby through to February of the next year, ending with Jewel's decision not to give up the baby to an institution.

I stopped the writing then, stunned at this rebellion, stymied at the loss of control of the subject. I stopped writing.

Only to have come to me in browsing through "The Nature and Aim of Fiction" one more time in preparation for teaching class (no student I teach ever emerges from one of my classes without reading this essay) the following passage, one I hadn't yet taken fully to heart for fear I would, in fact, never learn to write: "One thing that is always with the writer—no matter how long he has written or how good he is—is the continuing process of learning how to write. As soon as the writer 'learns to write,' as soon as he knows what he is going to find, and discovers a way to say what he knew all along, or worse still, a way to say nothing, he is finished. If a writer is any good, what he makes will have its source in a realm much larger than that which his conscious mind can encompass and will always be a greater surprise to him than it can ever be to his reader."

We want technique, I discovered only then—How many times had I read this passage before? How many?—because we fear the future. We have been to the future, operate here every day, and we know it to be messy. Unpredictable. Frightening, because it is out of our control. Technique, we figure, will help us in our predictions of the future. Knowing fictive techniques will help us make what hasn't yet been made easier to make. It will make the future neat for us, and predictable, and in our control, and so that future will, through the glory of technique, be less frightening, and therefore less intimidating.

But it is the inherent frightening and intimidating nature of the creation of art that makes the *discovery* the reward of art, and the reward to the artist, I heard O'Connor say that day. The predictable future is the future the true artist can live without. It is precisely the unforeseeable moment of discovery that in fact fuels the desire of the true artist and hence fuels true art.

The truth will be arrived at only through arriving at it. ✓ This will only be how you will know technique.

O'Connor's words have also been as true for the art of creative nonfiction as for the art of fiction, though the term creative nonfiction is something I am certain she would laugh over were she to hear it spoken as casually and seriously as it is today. *Fathers, Sons and Brothers* began not as a memoir—that decision was made by my agent when, after the book had been turned down several times, she decided to change the title page from *Fathers, Sons and Brothers: Personal Essays* to *Fathers, Sons and Brothers: A Memoir,* the next publisher to see it then buying it—nor did it begin even as a group of personal essays. The term creative nonfiction was something I'd never heard of when the writing of the book began, way back again in 1984, back when I was that instructor of remedial English at Ohio State. That first quarter—it couldn't have been but days after I'd watched that episode of *Dallas* during which my writing education truly began—the head of the department mandated that all faculty write an essay for the next departmental meeting so that we could feel firsthand what we were expecting of our students, and so be better teachers.

An essay? I'd been writing them all through high school, college, and grad school: the M.F.A. from the University of Massachusetts then was made up of the same number of academic hours as the Ph.D., and so we M.F.A. people took the same classes as the Ph.D.s, and wrote and were evaluated by the same standards. I'd written essays before. And my identification with my students didn't need to be any deeper: I'd been writing every day by then for four years, had just finished my M.F.A. thesis, was launched upon a novel. Empathy for my students? Come on.

But it was an assignment, and I had to do it.

And it just so happened that Zeb, a little over one and speaking quite well, upon waking each morning would call out "Mommy!" first thing, no matter that Melanie and I had worked out an even-steven system of tending to him each day, one day me the first to go in there, change his diaper, get him going, the next day Melanie.

But that didn't matter to Zeb—the same guy who picked up that smaller, sobbing scout's backpack and carried it up a mountain, but only after he'd checked on me—because every morning Zeb cried out "Mommy!" whether it was me or Melanie to answer him.

A fact which, at the time, bothered me: I was Mommy in the mornings, though he'd eventually get around to calling me Daddy sometime later in the day. But the first one through his door, the first one to respond each morning, was Mommy, whether I liked it or not.

So I wrote an essay about this strange fact of identity, of parenthood, of duty and obligation no matter the name you were given.

And promptly put it away, once it had been turned in and assessed by the head of the department as "cute." But its writing had taught me something: there were things—factual things—going on in my own life that deserved my attention as a writer, things that, once the scrim of fiction had been raised to reveal I was left with the *fact* of people I knew and loved, I might want to write about.

Because the essay about my son calling me Mommy gave me, in the writing of it, a *discovery* about the truth of who I am as a parent: it didn't matter what he called me. He needed me, and loved me, and I him. This gift of grace bestowed upon me by my own son was a point I had not thought of when I began writing the piece, when I began it as only an assignment. Back then it was simply an odd moment out of my life I believed worth looking at a little more closely, yielding, unbidden by me, this discovery.

Bearing out for me the truth of O'Connor's observation regarding the making of art, and the tentative and rock-hard alliance that grace and nature—that is, love and the willingness to stare long enough to see it—must have in order to find art: "St. Thomas called art 'reason in making'," she writes again in "The Nature and Aim of Fiction." "This is a very cold and very beautiful definition, and if it is unpopular today, this is because reason has lost ground among us. As grace and nature have been separated, so imagination and reason have been separated, and this always means an end to art. The artist uses his reason to discover an answering reason in everything he sees. For him, to be reasonable is to find, in the object, in the situation, in the sequence, the spirit which makes it itself. This is not an easy or simple thing to do. It is to intrude upon the timeless, and that is only done by the violence of a single-minded respect for the truth."

Thus began the memoir, though it would be nine years before it would be anywhere near a book, as over those nine years I simply sat down now and again and wrote the fact of what was happening with my children, and my *perceptions of* that fact. I found in what I saw associations between the often numskull things they were doing and the *always* numskull things I and my own brothers did as we were growing up, and associations as well with stories I had heard of the *profoundly* numskull things my father and his brothers did to one another growing up. "But there's a certain grain of stupidity that the writer of fiction can hardly do without, and this is the quality of having to stare, of not getting the point at once" begins "The Nature and Aim of Fiction." Not often enough do we get to read the rest of that thought, its explication by the one who taught me to see: "The longer you look at one object," she goes on, "the more of the world you see in it; and it's well to remember that the serious fiction writer always writes about the whole world, no matter how limited his particular scene. For him, the bomb that was dropped on Hiroshima affects life on the Oconee River, and there's not anything he can do about it."

And here were essays, true stories, about the nature of men, about the nature of family, about the nature of love, all of them unintended when I embarked upon writing them, and all of them put in a drawer because the discoveries each piece yielded—about who I was and who my siblings and children and father all were—were reward enough for the writing, until one day I pulled one of those essays from the drawer, one written about a year before and simply collecting that proverbial dust. I read it, liked it, shrugged, and decided to send it to a journal, *Antioch Review*.

And Robert Fogarty took it. And then I started sending other essays out, and writing more, the idea now finally taking shape back in the brain that perhaps this could be a book.

Nothing I knew would ever happen—nothing I even considered—when first I sat down to write that assignment.

I know nothing.

"A gift of any kind is a considerable responsibility," O'Connor writes in "On Her Own Work." "It is a mystery in itself, something gratuitous and wholly undeserved, something whose real uses will probably always be hidden from us.

Usually the artist has to suffer certain deprivations in order to use his gift with integrity. Art is a virtue of the practical intellect, and the practice of any virtue demands a certain asceticism and a very definite leaving-behind of the niggardly part of the ego. The writer has to judge himself with a stranger's eye and a stranger's severity. The prophet in him has to see the freak. No art is sunk in the self, but rather, in art the self becomes self-forgetful in order to meet the demands of the thing seen and the thing being made."

What I have come to know through this continuous wrestling with the gift of the habit of art—through, finally, my life—is that I must strip myself of all notions of what I believe and know about the world and the way it works. But once the individual gives up these notions of knowing a thing or two, all *prejudices* about the world, he is left with a *new* world, which is, of course, and paradoxically, the same old one.

Yet now it's new terrain, undiscovered, left to this new explorer, the one who knows nothing and who now, armed with this ignorance, stupidity, and tendency to stare, sees things freshly, and realizes, again if he is lucky, that staring is indeed a virtuous act, containing in its seemingly passive action all the elements necessary to understanding. "The writer should never be ashamed of staring." O'Connor elaborates upon that grain of stupidity. "There is nothing that doesn't require his attention."

What this explorer will ultimately discover is his or her own heart, who he or she is in the midst of all the know-it-alls of the world. Because this is what I am after in all this knowing of nothing: finding out who, in fact, I am.

Even now I can't attribute this notion of surrendering the will to find the truth only to O'Connor, but I find in her words the echo of an even greater and more profound truth, as it was

Christ who gave us this supreme of paradoxes: "For whoever wishes to save his life will lose it; but whoever loses his life for my sake and the gospel's shall save it. For what does it profit a man to gain the whole world, and forfeit his soul?"

Which is why it scares me to be here and writing this about a writer as important as O'Connor, as though I am some sort of possessor of the mystery of what it means to be a writer. It means having children in Boy Scouts, and it means a wife I can't figure out. And it means, too, the books I have written, though they come way down on the list. They are only crude maps of the worlds I've done my best to walk through, rough charts of the seas I've done my best to navigate. And still I know nothing.

Because there is, finally, no such thing as the writer. There is only this, the wellspring not only of the art of fiction, but the habit of being altogether: the simple act and art of paying attention.

It is the wellspring, I believe, because it is *paying attention* that can then become, in the strange and unpredictable alchemy of the mind, *experience;* experience is then sifted through the heart into *perception;* perception is then burnished by the soul into *understanding;* and it will be understanding, through the colossal and unfathomable compression of the writer's solitude and tenacity and fearless faith in the intuitive, that will yield finally, like diamonds from coal, the inescapable truth of *you.*

This is the gift of O'Connor's words, the mystery of her mannered essays on the act of writing, these pieces illuminating for us all that, without the consciousness of the artist— without the unique being who sees the human condition we all see each day of our lives through the singular window behind which we stand—there can be no art.

And perhaps the only true way I can come near to articulating this appreciation for O'Connor and her words is to reckon myself to the fact that in spite of the books I have written—and I truly mean *in spite of* because each book written gives me the foolish belief that I know how to write, when I'm damned if the next one doesn't provide its own set of problems that I alone must solve with the aid of *Mystery and Manners,* my Rosetta Stone—in spite of all those books, I continually try to find the limits and possibilities of words and try to accord them the respect they are due.

I am only trying to tell a story and, in the telling of it, find its meaning.

The end of this story is that my boys did precisely what I said they did at the outset of this all: Zeb carried that second backpack, Jacob gave me that water. And fool that I am, I did, what I said I did as well: I gave my kids a stern lecture; I stumbled exhausted into camp, the last man up; I drained my younger son's last drop of water.

Then we hiked another day, and another, and we went home, climbed into our warm beds, and slept.

But in the middle of that night, me sore, bleary with exhaustion, I woke up, thirsty, and went for a glass of water. Then I had no choice but to think of my son giving me water, and had no choice as well but to see my older son carrying a backpack up the mountain and to see him turning first to check on me.

Only now do I see the gift they have both given me. Not the look at me, Zeb's checking on me, and not Jake's last dribble of water. The true gift, the one I am only now realizing as I write this now—for the purposes of an appreciation of Flannery O'Connor—is the memory I have of them giving those gifts, the picture in my head of twin momentary beneficences that will last as long as I have memory. My gift back to them, the gesture (however small and egotistical and rife with my own ignorance) is my writing this discovery down for you, right now.

Here is the mystery, revealed through and with and yet transcending the manners of the story—the texture of wind through trees, of sweat and mountain air and aching muscles—to let me touch, finally, upon grace: the gestures, totally unexpected and totally right, of a nod and a second backpack, of the gift to an ignorant father of the last drops of water.

A gift for which O'Connor has done her best to teach me the responsibility for and to: the Divine life and our participation in it.

Bret Lott

Nineteen

Talking to Flannery

There was a time when critics compared new Southern writers, if male, with William Faulkner, while females were given two options by whom they could be outclassed. If philosophically inclined to Athens, they were measured against Eudora Welty; the slightest whiff of theocentric Jerusalem meant that Flannery O'Connor would become the plumbline.

With me that early religious whiff was slight indeed, and at a reviewer's first mention that I might be in O'Connor's camp, I was so ignorant that not only had I failed to read her work; if asked, I'd have said I had not read *his*.

Chronologically she was only seven years older than I. *Wise Blood* came out the year before I published my first collegiate story in *Mademoiselle* magazine. After a scalding encounter with Hazel Motes and Hoover Shoats, I knew with humility that more than years separated us; like the biblical number seven, she was wholly different, wholly mature. Beside her I felt not only pale but shrunken like Enoch's mummy.

In those years I was gradually giving up on last-gasp Christianity, backing away via Barth, Brunner, and Niebuhr, as, one by one, their new definitions failed me, then relinquishing more territory with Jung, and at last updating Marcus Aurelius with Camus. I was turning into the very type O'Connor liked least: a Julian, a Hulga-Joy, an Asbury Fox.

Ordinary details confirmed our contrast. She, Catholic. I, a Calvinist gone (*ascended*, I thought then) beyond agnostic. I was married, healthy, with children and a job; she had lupus and rural isolation and *that mother*. As an elected school board member in Sanford, North Carolina, I was working for school integration; for O'Connor, civil rights had been subsumed under eternal verities. "A Good Man Is Hard to Find" reminded me of too many sermons in the Associate Reformed Presbyterian Church from which I'd fled; in preachers' anecdotes there was always a moment when some death-row convict said with fervor, "why if I believed that about Jesus Christ, I would crawl across England on broken glass in order to. . ." and so on.

Been there, heard that.

Then my best friend, Louise Hardeman Abbot (another *Mademoiselle* prizewinner) left Chapel Hill for Louisville, Georgia, and met and frequently visited O'Connor at Andalusia. I learned that we both read with fascination a fundamentalist harangue published as a display ad in newspapers in Atlanta and Raleigh, "Why Do the Heathen Rage?" And we were both highly amused by Dr. Crane's tinkertoy psychology column, which I proofread for the *Sanford Herald*.

Once Louise showed her new friend a few of my stories. The reaction was polite but not admiring; O'Connor implied that an essential element was missing. I already knew how many elements were not there, feared they never would be. Certainly my characters earned no Damascus-road interventions, and by then it was clear to me that Paul had either hysteria or epilepsy.

In 1964 Louise wrote me about visiting O'Connor in the hospital, then grieved over her death at only thirty-nine. I believe I was more sad for Louise than Flannery, still an abstraction to me, a literary talent gone too soon.

Soon after, when our third child entered first grade, I began teaching at UNC-Chapel Hill and now started reading O'Connor's work as a teacher ("straining the soup too thin") but also as a writer who used her stories in the classroom.

My mentor in that English Department, the late C. Hugh Holman, told me about taking Katherine Anne Porter to Andalusia. After they had seen peacocks and other poultry and were resting with cool drinks indoors, Porter asked if there were never any problems with marauding dogs. O'Connor drew a drapery aside and from behind it lifted a leaning—rifle or shotgun. She sighted down the barrel through the window glass. "Not any more," she allegedly said, and then replaced the gun. Later Hugh drove a silent Porter quite a long way from the farmhouse while she stared blankly through the windshield, at last turning to say to him with a sigh, "That woman scares me to death."

Was this story true? Apocryphal? In *The Habit of Being* I find only that in March of 1958 Porter came with the Gossets and "two professors from North Carolina."

Perhaps he told me because he sensed that in some ways Flannery O'Connor scared me to death as well. Jill P. Baumgaertner, in her study *A Proper Scaring*, asks in her preface, "How could prose simultaneously make me laugh and scare me so deeply?"

Today "Greenleaf" scares me still, its outcome more like Zeus to Europa than Christ to Mary Magdalene.

While teaching O'Connor to undergraduates who were less scared than baffled, I discovered three things: (1) All over the Bible Belt, Sunday School was *out*, at least the Sunday School I had known. Samson and Goliath and Daniel were all missing from students' allusion index; they had never bent to darken a catechism page; grace would in the future have to reach most of them by computer or video game. (2) White students didn't understand why African American students giggled with glee over Julian's self-conscious liberalism on the bus. White students criticized what blacks understood about the historical defense mechanisms at work when Randall and Morgan ran their fake shuffle by Asbury in "The Enduring Chill." And (3) I learned not to assign students more than one or two of these stories at a time. My one weekend assignment of a whole O'Connor collection brought in on Monday morning a glassy-eyed classroom more displaced than Mr. Guizac.

But something else was happening to me, too—a shift in vision less extreme than for many of her characters, but still enough to turn her prose translucent, with shadowed depths beyond each word. I wanted to lift the book and shake out a dark lump of mystery under the reading lamp.

Reading O'Connor, my eye had dropped its academic scales, and I was acquiring again that old Biblical eye that had not quite offended me sufficiently to be put out.

Oh, sometimes I argued that art should not need scripture, and no doubt Joyce and Eliot could have dispensed with their referential frameworks also, but I could not keep the old memorized cadences of the 23rd Psalm out of "The Lame Shall Enter First," nor the Gadarene swine out of

"Revelation," nor Acts 2 out of that ceiling stain, nor the Pharisee and Publican out of almost everything *she* wrote— and a few fictions, like *Heading West*, of my own.

And although I haven't admitted this in public before now, I had begun to talk to Flannery O'Connor, under my breath often, sometimes even out loud. This monologue started about 1969 after her clear and unambiguous voice in *Mystery and Manners* talked so straight to me. Thereafter, a ludicrously prideful incident on campus, a casual blasphemy anywhere, Carl Sagan on TV, would make me mutter, "Did you hear that, Flannery?" with a roll of the eyes overhead, plus occasionally a low *heehaaw* noise that was half peahen and half ass. Sometimes now I apologize to her for having had thirty-two more years than she, nearly double hers, and having done so little. And now that my mother, eighty-five, lives with us, I sometimes comment on Southern women of all ages. Still, my view of Regina has grown affectionate, in full knowledge of the normal aggravations and hilarities of normal families.

By the time *The Habit of Being* arrived in 1979, all of us readers were able to mourn the tough-minded, warm-hearted, humorous woman she was, and I joined the thousands of other mini-Pharisees who read her letters thinking, "'A'? When she could have been writing to *me*?"

In 1980, I went back to the church, though not to Flannery's Mother Church. I told her, aside, "My mama is deathly opposed to the Pope and his idols, you understand." I believe that she, who today would be seventy-five, understood.

Some of my favorite stories were written near her end, though not preferred because of that literary necrophilia, such as that sometimes awarded Plath and Sexton: Parker, with the image of God worn outside; poor Ruby Turpin,

learning that the last shall be first and the first last, with a
final paragraph that soars like Blakes' Job engravings; the
title story, in which Julian and I and all other Pharisees converge. If I prefer the stories to the novels, that's because each
delivers a sharp knockout punch while Motes and Tarwater
leave me more gradually bruised and still inclined to wiggle
free. I continue that "constant spiritual temperature-taking"
O'Connor warned against.

As even the Apostles, however united, were widely different temperamentally (John from Thomas, for example), I
have been telling O'Connor's spirit—aloud—that while for
some members of a secular audience she needed to shout and
draw large and startling pictures, we mothers and kinder-
garten teachers sometimes find a whisper reaches others in
the crowd. There's an unbroken line from the startling stories in scripture to hers, where Georgia piedmont bushes
may burst into flame (Moses to Parker) and rivers may heal
(Nathan to Harry Ashfield) and creatures may signify
(Balaam's ass to peacocks.)

But my characters won't recognize The Misfit until several
pages beyond "The End," and then only in some readers'
heads. Mine (Job's second-cousins-once-removed) don't get
their questions answered or even overwhelmed; if they come
close to the point of admitting "Mine eye seeth Thee," in
another minute they'll whisper, "That *is* You, isn't it?"

And Grace hasn't usually laid a glove on my characters at
the end; it is just climbing into the ring. They go back to ordinary lives barely beginning to accept the possibility that God
may be alive and well, though not yet as near as the treeline.

"So there's still an element missing?" I ask of my unstained
ceiling overhead. Dove, eagle, buzzard: none of them comes
down.

But listen, Flannery. I'm all the way to the end and one thing at least. One thing. Are you listening? I didn't once say *sub specie aeternetatis!*

Maybe a plaster flake or two. Cool.

Doris Betts

Twenty

Andalusia Visit

for Bill Sessions

Look out! my nightmare shouted,
as she crashed across the porch, flailing the shadows with a crutch.
Dark wind blew a storm of dust, or feathers, and lightning
through the rusted screen
flared off the lenses of her glasses.
You're not Billy, she said, jerking around twice,
rolling her neck like a peacock . . .

but the room had collected,
and that first filmy light through the curtains of the French doors
offered only my familiar brass and tarnished footboard,
the spool-backed rocker, the sunburst afghan
my dog had chewed into a rag . . .

No, wherever the dream had swept me,
someone else had been expected,

and I remembered she'd written:
I went to Communion for your intentions on Friday the 8th
and have been praying for you since.
Coming into the Church must have its terrors . . .

Terrors? Yes, and oddly that lightened my own.
Somehow in the dream I had stumbled
into another man's afternoon
another man's storm, but had come back startled and blessed,
the way someone leaving confession might slip
into the wrong raincoat
and find himself walking an unfamiliar street,
the clouds departed, the stars above the brownstones
more passionate than neon,
his head clearing,
his pockets bulging with possibility.

David Bottoms

Contributors

DORIS BETTS is Chancellor of the Fellowship of Southern Writers and Alumni Distinguished Professor at the University of North Carolina at Chapel Hill. She is a celebrated novelist and short story writer, and her works include *Beasts of the Southern Wild and Other Stories* (1973) and *The Sharp Teeth of Love* (1997).

DAVID BOTTOMS is a professor of English at Georgia State University and co-editor of *Five Points: A Journal of Literature and Art*. He has published five collections of poetry including *Vagrant Grace* (1999) and a novel, *Easter Weekend* (1990). Bottoms' numerous awards include the Walt Whitman Award for Poetry and an Ingram-Merrill Award.

MARY WARD BROWN lives on a three-hundred-acre farm in Marion Junction, Alabama, where she has lived for most of her life. She received the 1987 PEN/Ernest Hemingway Foundation Award for her first short story collection *Tongues of Flame* (1986).

ANDREA HOLLANDER BUDY is the author of two full-length collections of poetry: *House Without A Dreamer* (1993), which won the Nicholas Roerich Poetry Prize, and *The Other Life* (2000). She lives in Mountain Bluff, Arkansas.

FRED CHAPPELL is the celebrated author of numerous works of criticism, fiction, and poetry, including the novels, *I Am One of You Forever* (1985) and *Look Back All the Green Valley* (1999). His volumes of poetry include *Spring Garden: New and Selected Poems* (1995). Chappell is a founding member of the Fellowship of Southern Writers and has been awarded the T. S. Eliot Prize of the Ingersoll Foundation and the Bollingen Prize in poetry, along with many other honors.

ROBERT COLES is professor of Psychiatry and Medical Humanities at Harvard Medical School, co-editor of *DoubleTake* magazine, and the author of more than sixty books, including the five volume *Children of Crisis* (1967–77), for which he won a Pulitzer Prize. His other works include *Flannery O'Connor's South* (1980), *The Spiritual Life of Children* (1990), and *The Secular Mind* (1999). In 1999 President Clinton awarded Coles the Presidential Medal of Freedom, the nation's highest civilian honor.

SARAH GORDON is editor of *The Flannery O'Connor Bulletin* and an internationally known O'Connor scholar. She has taught English at Georgia College & State University, O'Connor's alma mater, for over twenty-five years. Her works include a poetry collection, *Distances* (1999), and a critical study *Flannery O'Connor: The Obedient Imagination* (2000).

SUSAN ELIZABETH HOWE has served as the editor of several journals, including *Exponent II*. Howe received the Association for Mormon Letters Award in poetry for her poetry collection, *Stone Spirits* (1997). Her work has appeared in numerous magazines, including *The New Yorker*.

MARK JARMAN is a professor of English at Vanderbilt University and is the author of five collections of poetry, including *Black Riviera* (1990) and *Questions for Ecclesiastes*, which won the 1998 Lenore Marshall Poetry Prize.

GREG JOHNSON has garnered critical acclaim with his short story collections, including *Distant Friends* (1990) and *I Am Dangerous* (1996). He received the O. Henry Prize Award in 1986. His other works include a novel, *Pagan Babies* (1993) and *Invisible Writer* (1998), the authorized biography of Joyce Carol Oates.

MADISON JONES, novelist, short story writer and critic, is professor emeritus of English and writer-in-residence at Auburn University. His many works include the novels, *A Cry of Absence* (1971) and *Nashville 1864: The Dying of the Light* (1997), which won the Michael Shaara Award. Jones has been awarded several fellowships, including grants from the Guggenheim Foundation, the Rockefeller Foundation, and the *Sewanee Review*.

MAXINE KUMIN is the author of eleven volumes of poetry, including *Connecting the Dots* (1996) and *Up Country: Poems of New England* (1972), for which she won the Pulitzer Prize. She is also a novelist, essayist, short story writer, and the author of more than twenty children's books. Kumin is a former Chancellor of the Academy of American Poets and her numerous awards include the Levinson Prize and a National Endowment for the Arts grant.

BRET LOTT is the author of several novels and short story collections, including *Jewel* (1991), *Reed's Beach* (1993), and *The Hunt Club* (1998). He has also written a memoir, *Fathers, Sons and Brothers* (1997). Lott has received a syndicated fiction project award from PEN/National Endowment for the Arts and a South Carolina Arts Commission fellowship in literature. He is writer-in-residence and professor of English at the College of Charleston in Charleston, South Carolina.

DAVID MADDEN is the author of numerous works of fiction and nonfiction, including the short story collection *The New Orleans of Possibilities* (1982) and the novels, *Cassandra Singing* (1969) and *Sharpshooter: A Novel of the Civil War* (1996). Madden has been awarded a Rockefeller grant, the John Golden fellowship in playwriting at Yale University, and the National Endowment for the Arts fiction prize.

NANCY MAIRS is a celebrated essayist, whose most recent essay collection is *Waist-High in the World: A Life Among the Nondisabled* (1996), an autobiographical account of her struggle with multiple sclerosis. Her other works include *Remembering the Bone House: An Erotics of Place and Space* (1989) and *Carnal Acts* (1990).

PADGETT POWELL is the author of five books of fiction, including the novels *Edisto* (1984) and *Edisto: Revisited* (1996). His short stories have won critical acclaim, and he has published two story collections, *Typical* (1991) and *Aliens of Affection* (1998). Powell has received the Prix de Rome of the American Academy of Arts and Letters and a Whiting Writer's Award. He teaches at the University of Florida.

LEE SMITH has published more than a dozen novels and short story collections, including *Cakewalk* (1980), *Fair and Tender Ladies* (1988), and *News of the Spirit* (1997). Smith is a member of the Fellowship of

Southern Writers, and she was awarded the first Chubb LifeAmerica
Award in honor of Robert Penn Warren.

GUERRILLA GIRL ALMA THOMAS is the pseudonym of an
African American visual artist. The Guerrilla Girls, founded in New
York in 1985, is a group of women artists, writers, performers, film-
makers, and arts professionals with the explicit mission of protesting
racism, sexism, and classism in the art world. Members of this direct-
action group keep their identities secret and wear gorilla masks during
demonstrations to focus on issues rather than on personalities.

KELLIE WELLS teaches creative writing at Georgia College & State
University, O'Connor's alma mater, and has published short stories in
a number of journals, including *Prairie Schooner*. She received special
mention for two stories in *The Pushcart Prize: Best of the Small Presses
1999*. Wells is currently at work on a novel.

MILLER WILLIAMS, one of America's best-loved poets, teaches at
the University of Arkansas and is Director of the University of
Arkansas Press. His most recent book of poetry is *Some Jazz a While:
Collected Poems* (1999). Winner of the National Arts Award in 1997,
Williams was President Clinton's choice for Inaugural Poet in 1997.

An O'Connor Chronology

1925   Mary Flannery born on March 25 to Edward Francis and Regina
Cline O'Connor in Savannah, Georgia

1942   Graduated from Peabody High School, Milledgeville, Georgia

1942–45   Attended Georgia State College for Women, Milledgeville, and
received a B.A. in Social Science.

1945–47   Attended the Writers' Workshop, State University of Iowa, and
received an M.F.A.

1946   First published story, "The Geranium," *Accent, 6,* Summer 1946

1952   First published novel, *Wise Blood*

1953   "The Life You Save May Be Your Own," *Prize Stories 1954: The O.
Henry Awards*

1954   "A Circle in the Fire," *Prize Stories 1955: The O. Henry Awards*
and *The Best American Short Stories of 1955*

1954–55   Fellowship in fiction, *Kenyon Review*

1955   First published collection of short stories, *A Good Man Is Hard to Find*

1956   "Greenleaf," *Prize Stories 1957: The O. Henry Awards* (first prize story)
and *The Best American Short Stories of 1957*

1957   "A View of the Woods," *The Best American Short Stories of 1958*
Grant from the National Institute of Arts and Letters

1959   Grant from the Ford Foundation

1960   Second published novel, *The Violent Bear It Away*

1962   "Everything That Rises Must Converge," *The Best American Short
Stories of 1962*

1963   "Everything that Rise Must Converge," *Prize Stories 1963: The O.
Henry Awards* (first prize story)

1964   Henry Bellaman Foundation Award
Flannery O'Connor died on August 3 in Milledgeville

1965   Second published collection of short stories, *Everything That Rises
Must Converge*
"Revelation," *Prize Stories 1965: The O. Henry Awards* (first prize story)

1969   *Mystery and Manners: Occasional Prose* published

1971   *The Complete Stories* published
Winner, National Book Award

1979   *The Habit of Being: Letters of Flannery O'Connor* published

1983   *The Presence of Grace and Other Book Reviews by Flannery O'Connor*
published

1989   *Flannery O'Connor: Collected Works* published